HEL

Sally Raymond is married witl
whom is dyslexic. She also
recent years, she obtained th
teaching of children with specific learning
achieving a distinction for her st
herself as
and is an active member of a local parent and teacher
dyslexia support group. Her activity book *Treasure Hunt*
(Henderson, 1995) published material she used to support
her daughter's specific learning needs, and reflects her
interest in using games as learning resources.

Overcoming Common Problems Series

For a full list of titles please contact
Sheldon Press, Marylebone Road, London NW1 4DU

The Assertiveness Workbook
A plan for busy women
JOANNA GUTMANN

Beating the Comfort Trap
DR WINDY DRYDEN AND JACK
GORDON

Birth Over Thirty Five
SHEILA KITZINGER

Body Language
How to read others' thoughts by their
gestures
ALLAN PEASE

Body Language in Relationships
DAVID COHEN

Calm Down
How to cope with frustration and anger
DR PAUL HAUCK

Cancer – A Family Affair
NEVILLE SHONE

The Candida Diet Book
KAREN BRODY

Caring for Your Elderly Parent
JULIA BURTON-JONES

Comfort for Depression
JANET HORWOOD

Coping Successfully with Hayfever
DR ROBERT YOUNGSON

Coping Successfully with Migraine
SUE DYSON

Coping Successfully with Pain
NEVILLE SHONE

Coping Successfully with PMS
KAREN EVENNETT

Coping Successfully with Panic Attacks
SHIRLEY TRICKETT

**Coping Successfully with Prostate
Problems**
ROSY REYNOLDS

**Coping Successfully with Your
Hyperactive Child**
DR PAUL CARSON

**Coping Successfully with Your Irritable
Bowel**
ROSEMARY NICOL

**Coping Successfully with Your Second
Child**
FIONA MARSHALL

Coping with Anxiety and Depression
SHIRLEY TRICKETT

Coping with Blushing
DR ROBERT EDELMANN

Coping with Breast Cancer
DR EADIE HEYDERMAN

Coping with Bronchitis and Emphysema
DR TOM SMITH

Coping with Candida
SHIRLEY TRICKETT

Coping with Chronic Fatigue
TRUDIE CHALDER

Coping with Crushes
ANITA NAIK

Coping with Cystitis
CAROLINE CLAYTON

Coping with Depression and Elation
DR PATRICK McKEON

Coping with Eczema
DR ROBERT YOUNGSON

Coping with Endometriosis
JO MEARS

Coping with Psoriasis
PROFESSOR RONALD MARKS

Coping with Schizophrenia
DR STEVEN JONES AND DR FRANK
TALLIS

Coping with Stomach Ulcers
DR TOM SMITH

Coping with Thyroid Problems
DR JOAN GOMEZ

Coping with Thrush
CAROLINE CLAYTON

Coping with Your Cervical Smear
KAREN EVENNETT

Crunch Points for Couples
JULIA COLE

Curing Arthritis Exercise Book
MARGARET HILLS AND JANET
HORWOOD

Overcoming Common Problems Series

Curing Arthritis Diet Book
MARGARET HILLS

Curing Arthritis – The Drug-Free Way
MARGARET HILLS

Curing Arthritis
More ways to a drug-free life
MARGARET HILLS

Curing Illness – The Drug-Free Way
MARGARET HILLS

Depression
DR PAUL HAUCK

Divorce and Separation
Every woman's guide to a new life
ANGELA WILLANS

Everything Parents Should Know About Drugs
SARAH LAWSON

Gambling – A Family Affair
ANGELA WILLANS

Good Stress Guide, The
MARY HARTLEY

Heart Attacks – Prevent and Survive
DR TOM SMITH

Helping Children Cope with Bullying
SARAH LAWSON

Helping Children Cope with Divorce
ROSEMARY WELLS

Helping Children Cope with Grief
ROSEMARY WELLS

Helping Children Cope with Stammering
DR TRUDIE STEWART AND JACKIE TURNBULL

Hold Your Head Up High
DR PAUL HAUCK

How to Be Your Own Best Friend
DR PAUL HAUCK

How to Cope when the Going Gets Tough
DR WINDY DRYDEN AND JACK GORDON

How to Cope with Bulimia
DR JOAN GOMEZ

How to Cope with Difficult Parents
DR WINDY DRYDEN AND JACK GORDON

How to Cope with Difficult People
ALAN HOUEL WITH CHRISTIAN GODEFROY

How to Cope with Splitting Up
VERA PEIFFER

How to Cope with Stress
DR PETER TYRER

How to Enjoy Your Retirement
VICKY MAUD

How to Improve Your Confidence
DR KENNETH HAMBLY

How to Interview and Be Interviewed
MICHELE BROWN AND GYLES BRANDRETH

How to Keep Your Cholesterol in Check
DR ROBERT POVEY

How to Love and Be Loved
DR PAUL HAUCK

How to Pass Your Driving Test
DONALD RIDLAND

How to Stand up for Yourself
DR PAUL HAUCK

How to Start a Conversation and Make Friends
DON GABOR

How to Stick to a Diet
DEBORAH STEINBERG AND DR WINDY DRYDEN

How to Stop Smoking
GEORGE TARGET

How to Stop Worrying
DR FRANK TALLIS

How to Survive Your Teenagers
SHEILA DAINOW

How to Untangle Your Emotional Knots
DR WINDY DRYDEN AND JACK GORDON

How to Write a Successful CV
JOANNA GUTMANN

Hysterectomy
SUZIE HAYMAN

The Incredible Sulk
DR WINDY DRYDEN

The Irritable Bowel Diet Book
ROSEMARY NICOL

The Irritable Bowel Stress Book
ROSEMARY NICOL

Is HRT Right for You?
DR ANNE MacGREGOR

Jealousy
DR PAUL HAUCK

Learning to Live with Multiple Sclerosis
DR ROBERT POVEY, ROBIN DOWIE AND GILLIAN PRETT

Living with Angina
DR TOM SMITH

Overcoming Common Problems Series

Living with Asthma
DR ROBERT YOUNGSON

Living with Diabetes
DR JOAN GOMEZ

Living with Grief
DR TONY LAKE

Living with High Blood Pressure
DR TOM SMITH

Making the Most of Yourself
GILL FOX AND SHEILA DAINOW

Menopause
RAEWYN MACKENZIE

Migraine Diet Book, The
SUE DYSON

Motor Neurone Disease – A Family Affair
DR DAVID OLIVER

The Nervous Person's Companion
DR KENNETH HAMBLY

Out of Work – A Family Affair
ANNE LOVELL

Overcoming Anger
DR WINDY DRYDEN

Overcoming Guilt
DR WINDY DRYDEN

Overcoming Stress
DR VERNON COLEMAN

The Parkinson's Disease Handbook
DR RICHARD GODWIN-AUSTEN

The PMS Diet Book
KAREN EVENNETT

Serious Mental Illness – A Family Affair
GWEN HOWE

Sleep Like a Dream – The Drug-Free Way
ROSEMARY NICOL

Subfertility Handbook, The
VIRGINIA IRONSIDE AND SARAH
BIGGS

Talking About Anorexia
How to cope with life without starving
MAROUSHKA MONRO

Ten Steps to Positive Living
DR WINDY DRYDEN

Think Your Way to Happiness
DR WINDY DRYDEN AND JACK
GORDON

**Understanding Obsessions and
Compulsions**
A self-help manual
DR FRANK TALLIS

Understanding Your Personality
Myers-Briggs and more
PATRICIA HEDGES

A Weight Off Your Mind
How to stop worrying about your body size
SUE DYSON

When your Child Comes Out
ANNE LOVELL

Overcoming Common Problems

Helping Children Cope with Dyslexia

Sally Raymond

sheldon PRESS

First published in Great Britain in 1997 by
Sheldon Press, SPCK,
Marylebone Road,
London NW1 4DU

© Sally Raymond 1997

British Library Cataloguing-in-Publication Data
A catalogue record for this book is available from the British Library

ISBN 0–85969–772–X

Photoset by Deltatype Ltd, Birkenhead
Printed in Great Britain by
Biddles Ltd, Guildford and King's Lynn

To Rita and Graham

Contents

	Introduction	1
1	Putting a face to dyslexia	3
2	At home with dyslexia	10
3	Reading matters	20
4	Spelling issues	28
5	Mathematical concerns	39
6	Educational play	43
7	Schooling concerns	52
8	The wider world	64
9	Memory matters	68
10	Positive outlook	79
11	Activities	85
	Further reading	94
	Useful addresses	95
	Index	97

Introduction

'Dyslexia' is no longer an unusual word. Most of us can even spell it. However, 100 years ago they were calling it 'word-blindness' and its symptoms were only just becoming recognized.

Discovering your child is dyslexic is not easy. First, the learning pattern of dyslexic children is not exclusive to them, and may only be subtly disordered; so it may take months, or even years, before their difficulty is identified. Second, while the term 'dyslexia' is familiar, the details of the condition and the variability of its characteristics are not. A lack of information can put parents at a loss to know the whats, whys and wherefores associated with the announcement that their child is dyslexic (or has a 'specific learning difficulty', as it is sometimes called).

A 'specific learning difficulty' means a problem with learning particular things. In the case of dyslexics, it refers to the specific difficulty these individuals have with reading, writing and often arithmetic. The term 'specific' is used because these individuals do not show poor learning ability when mastering other skills; but only those skills largely associated with the handling and storing of symbolic material.

'Dyslexia' means a difficulty with words or language. This includes speech, grammar, meaning and rhyme, which in turn all rely heavily on the memory processes of the mind to be manipulated effectively. Anything which involves remembering a sequence of events can be difficult for a dyslexic: reciting the alphabet, tying shoelaces, working out a maths sum. And as fine motor control is often slow to develop, poor manipulation of footballs, pencils and eating utensils are frequently observed too.

It is worth noting that educational and scientific experts in the field of dyslexia are still contesting each other's explanations of the condition. While it is now accepted that it exists, dyslexia is seen to be so different between individuals that no one has been able to give one finite definition, or a clear understanding of its causes, symptoms and effects. In addition, there may be other difficulties such as untidy penmanship, confusion between left and right, poor focus of attention and/or a difficulty following instructions. The diversity of symptoms

1

may seem confusing to parents, but once they begin to understand the nature of their individual child, they will be better equipped to home in on their specific areas of difficulty and meet their individual needs. Some dyslexics are clumsy, others are not. Some can read but not spell. Others are (brilliant) mathematicians . . .

This book begins by introducing six dyslexic children who display varying degrees and types of dyslexic difficulties. By observing these children individually, and then within their homes, the reader can begin to identify with their predicaments, recognizing the subtle – sometimes devastating – effect dyslexia can have on their lives.

As parents uncover and understand their child's dyslexia within the home, confusions can be replaced with positive support. Reading, spelling, mathematics and play can all be handled in a positive manner, reducing the conflicts dyslexic difficulties can often cause.

At school, there are procedures and jargon to be understood. By knowing their individual child and their specific needs, parents are better equipped to understand and support the school. Through educated cooperation, teachers, parents and pupils can work together at achieving the best for the individual child.

By Chapter 8, the reader will be familiar with dyslexic difficulties, and able to support their child's enjoyment of the outside world; completing the passage from confusion to confidence in the home, at school and in the largely non-dyslexic world around them.

Three more chapters complete the main body of the book: 'Memory matters', which looks at the underlying causes of dyslexia; 'A positive outlook', with a self-explanatory title; and 'Activities', which includes such things as 'telling the time', 'learning the rules of -ing' and 'common words'.

A book such as this can only introduce a subject as complex as dyslexia. An appendix of names and addresses is included to help parents extend their knowledge further. By watching the media, new explanations, theories and teaching methods can be followed and understood.

1

Putting a face to dyslexia

*By recognizing your child's individual weaknesses, understanding
and progress can be made. By recognizing individual strengths and
ability, compensatory skills can be developed.*

By considering your child while reading the following pages, the
nature of their dyslexia will, hopefully, become more tangible. The
aim is to present you with a variety of dyslexic profiles, from which
you can begin to recognize your own child's individual areas of
specific weakness, as well as their strengths.

Through witnessing a variety of dyslexic children, and relating their
behaviour to specific learning difficulties, the nature of dyslexia is
brought to life. By following the development of these children
throughout the book – highlighting the effects, obstacles and solutions
that they face – specific learning difficulties can be understood even
further. This will help you to fashion support that meets the specific
needs of your own individual child.

Clare

Clare is ten years old. She is generally a cheerful child, with a younger
brother; but she struggles with reading, spelling and mathematics at
school, receiving extra support in English. Although Clare expresses
an understanding of the world about her and is always chattering, her
audiences are often frustrated by Clare's intermittent word-finding
difficulties, and lengthy tales that lack sequential structure. Clare likes
books (but prefers television), and has achieved a reading age of nine
years. But she often finds it hard to extract meaning from the text she
has just read.

For her birthday, Clare has received a stamp album and collection of
stamps. Attracted by the designs and colours of the stamps, Clare is
soon engrossed; but after fifteen minutes, she hurls the book and
stamps to the floor and runs upstairs, yelling abuse at everyone she
meets.

Jonathan

Jonathan is eight, and in year four at school. He started reading eagerly enough, but as the books became harder he regularly misread words – sometimes guessing at them wildly, sometimes reading them backwards. However, unlike Clare, Jonathan usually *does* extract meaning from the text so his guesses are sensible, even if they are incorrect. Jonathan's teacher has suggested Jonathan reads to his parents at home for at least fifteen minutes each day, but Jonathan no longer wants to read with them. He claims the books are boring. Conflicts regularly occur.

Jonathan's writing is untidy, immature and full of spelling mistakes. He seems to have plenty of ideas, but lacks the ability to commit them to paper, rarely finishing written tasks in the time allowed in class. His teacher has provided him with handwriting tasks to practise at home, but again, he is reluctant to do them, further increasing the tensions within the family.

Mark

Mark is four and attends a playgroup – where he loves running around with the other children, but hates settling down to do jigsaws or construction games. Described as a clumsy child, Mark is often knocking things over and tripping himself up. He seems to have no idea of rhythm, and despite being one of the older children in the group, still falters through the nursery rhymes and counting games that are regularly played. An eyesight test has not revealed any reason for Mark's frequent accidents, but a developmental check-up last month suggested his vocabulary skills were immature.

However, Mark does show exceptional theatrical talent and loves entertaining himself and his family with unusual plays. His parents wonder if all this escapism is wise, and with Christmas looming, they have to decide if a Batman suit is a sensible buy.

Samantha

Samantha is thirteen years old and is not achieving success. She has not settled in well at secondary school and continues to get poor marks in classwork despite her teachers' assurances that 'she could do better'. Her school records describe Samantha as a quiet child, but at home

Samantha is increasingly disruptive. Her parents dread the ever-increasing workload of homework that takes up most of Samantha's spare time, making her tired, irritable and unpleasant to be with.

Quite often, Samantha seems unable to remember homework instructions. This leads to frequent telephone calls to friends, which her parents believe is an avoidance tactic, supported by the fact that vital books are frequently left at school.

When reading, Samantha often breaks unknown words into individual letters rather than syllables, and then makes wildly incorrect guesses. However, once she has been told a word, she will then recognize it from page to page. She just seems unable to decode unknown words successfully herself.

Her parents remember that, as a young child, Samantha did struggle with her reading, but it was the 'easy' words that gave her most difficulty. Her reading ability then seemed to catch up with the rest of the class until now, at secondary school, she is once more asking for help to decode textbook questions, explanations or names.

Samantha's spelling ability has never been good, but her handwriting is neat, and her artistic talent boosts the overall presentation of her work. Her parents are now considering extra tuition outside school, but cannot agree on which topic(s) to tackle.

Christopher

Christopher is eight years old and cannot do maths. However, his reading is acceptable for his age and, apart from an untidy writing style, he seems to be doing well in all other subjects. Christopher's parents remember he used to enjoy counting stairs when he was younger, but for months the sequence of numbers was disordered with some of the numbers missed out. Christopher's father found maths difficult himself when he was at school, so can appreciate his son's struggles. However, when they try to do maths homework together, Christopher's performance is so poor that his father despairs. He is beginning to think his son is just lazy and not applying himself properly.

Tom

Tom is seven years old and can hardly write a word. He 'reads' to himself from books he is familiar with, but cannot match the words of the text precisely with his memory of the story. Although still young,

Tom's literacy development is way behind his peers, yet he shows a well-developed spoken vocabulary and an interest in stories. Tom also displays a skill that both surprises and confuses his parents: he seems to have an exceptionally good long-term memory. He can recall events from the past with clarity, yet he is unable to remember the spelling of a word from one day to the next.

When Tom joined Year Two, his teacher provided extra activities for him to do at home. Now his behaviour in class is beginning to deteriorate. Tummy aches are reported on weekdays, but they disappear when the weekend arrives. An appointment has been made, by the school, for Tom to be seen by an educational psychologist – a move which concerns his parents despite the assurance from the school that 'there is nothing to worry about'.

Pinpointing the characteristics of dyslexia

Clare, our wrathful stamp collector, is totally confused when faced with the unfamiliar symbols present on stamps. Her reading ability is only one year behind her chronological age, so she is achieving some literacy success; but she often reads without understanding the text before her.

These symptoms suggest that Clare is decoding words by breaking them down into their component sounds, for example, 'sh-op' (this is known as a phonological approach). But she seems unable to recognize whole words or symbolic representations of words (such as POLSKA found on stamps used in Poland) – achievements that rely on a visual memory of letter-patterns. Her phonological approach slows her reading down, burdening her brain with a laborious decoding technique. Challenged by the task of identifying the individual words within sentences, the overall meaning of the written piece becomes lost. Subtleties of punctuation confuse her. Any 'odd bods' (for example, the word 'because'), which do not follow standard sound-to-letter-group rules, distract her even further.

Jonathan's reading style is different from Clare's. He 'reads' quite fast, missing out words and confusing similarly spelled words with each other (what/that, went/want). When faced with an unknown word, he guesses at it rather than attempts to break it down into its component sounds. As his speed of reading is relatively fast, and he uses clues available from pictures surrounding the text, the meaning he

6

has gathered from the text can help his guesswork at difficult or confusing words by providing a predictive factor. This can also lead to mistakes, as words are missed out or displaced by others, altering the meaning Jonathan believes he is extracting with success.

While Clare attempts to decode words through a phonological approach, Jonathan is relying more on the visual aspects of words. These differences are also present in these children's spelling errors. Clare produces words that are spelled according to their sound (for example, 'mach' instead of 'match'). Jonathan attempts a visually based reproduction (for example, 'mtch'). Samantha also seems to be using her visual modality for spelling, but often reverses words too, so her contribution might be 'mhct'.

When reading, Samantha, even at thirteen years old, will still ask for a word rather than attempt to decode it herself. Sometimes she misreads words by substituting a word with a similar meaning: 'pretty' for 'beautiful', 'broken' for 'destroyed'. This suggests that Samantha is extracting meaning from the text as she reads, which is allowing her brain to provide 'contextual prompting'.

Contextual prompting encourages the brain to predict which words might come next. It also allows spoken language to 'flow' as associated words become available to the speaker. Clare's speech is disjointed and, when reading, she finds it hard to suggest the meaning of an unknown word, even if the surrounding text is understood.

Mark is only four, so is only just becoming aware of the written word. But with dyslexia already present in the family, Mark's parents worry about their son's developmental delays. They wonder if a similar lack of concentration, or interest in story books, counting games and colour identification, is the cause or effect of dyslexia in their older child who displayed a similar behavioural pattern in his early years.

Christopher had a traumatic arrival into this world. His parents wonder whether ante- and/or post-natal distress played a contributory part in their son's learning difficulties. Samantha's parents speculate as to whether their daughter's frequent bouts of 'glue ear' at infant school hampered her learning during vital years. Jonathan's parents argue about the level of pressure put upon him at home, fearing that attempts to improve their son's reading and writing skills have rendered him too insecure to relax and achieve success.

Any and all of these suggestions could be valid. They sound convincing, but we do hear of similar stories from parents whose children did not go on to develop specific difficulties in their learning. Although parents do worry about the *cause* of their children's difficulties, they also need to consider the *effect* dyslexic difficulties will have on their child. The fact is, the earlier dyslexia can be identified in the school-aged child, the better; so if a parent has any concern about the performance levels their child is achieving, they should not hesitate in contacting the school.

Christopher's specific difficulties seem to lie solely with mathematics. He can read well, has an acceptable spelling and writing ability and is rarely forgetful. He has been identified as lazy in maths because his performance in other areas of the curriculum is good, yet this enigma is not uncommon.

Dyslexic individuals can be relatively good readers and spellers but poor in maths, or they can be poor at reading and writing yet be *brilliant* mathematicians. And then there are different areas of maths, with some topics utilizing pattern, shape and comparison, while other branches of the subject involve number, sequential sums and transposition of symbolic data. Often, a lack of confidence in one area can be boosted with success in another.

Samantha is struggling with maths. It is quite possible that when she was at primary school, she had easier access to material supports and was not embarrassed to use her fingers. She may also have developed tactics or strategies to disguise her struggles. But at secondary school, the pressure of the environment and its extra demands means these deceptions are not enough to hide her misunderstandings.

Tom is anxious, and like many of the others, is facing failure at school at an early age, but he has also developed avoidance tactics (such as claiming illness to evade school). Tom actually does experience unpleasant feelings within his tummy when faced with stressful, challenging tasks, so his complaints are not unfounded. A visit to a doctor is prudent though, to ascertain there are no other causes for his discomfort.

Tactical behaviour is not uncommon among dyslexic children. Mark has discovered that by clapping his hands exceedingly loudly in time with the music, adults are only too keen to relieve him from the singing activities at playgroup that he hates. When Mark grows older, the same strategical thinking will help him discover that clapping (quietly) along with a song, will allow his hands to meter the beat, aiding his poor sense of rhythm.

Samantha has also developed a number of tactics to avoid or

8

decrease her difficulties. Her parents are right to suspect an element of deviousness in their daughter's homework-based disorganization. But behind Samantha's reluctance to tackle the tasks in hand, lies a difficulty she has with her working memory.

Jonathan displays this difficulty too: he has ideas for stories, begins to write, becomes overburdened by spelling demands and requests for neater penmanship. Then he forgets his story, or the sentence he wanted to write, or the word he was going to ask you how to spell.

A good working memory can sustain a number of messages simultaneously. A poor or overburdened working memory reduces the brain's ability to function well. By strategically reducing demands on the memory (such as showing Jonathan how he can briefly plan his story before tackling its detailed production), overloading of the working memory can be reduced.

Christopher is delighted to discover a tactic for reciting the nine times table with success. It involves the fingers displaying the pattern that exists due to the fact that each digital sum of the nine times table adds up to nine. Christopher holds up both hands with palms facing him. Counting the left thumb as 'finger one', he counts from left to right, folding down the fourth finger for 4×9. The resulting display is of three upright fingers to the left of the folded finger, and six to the right: $4 \times 9 = 36$. To calculate 6×9 he repeats the process, folding down the sixth finger from the left. The answer (54) can easily be 'read' off his fingers.

$1 \times 9 = 09 (0 + 9 = 9)$
$2 \times 9 = 18 (1 + 8 = 9)$
$3 \times 9 = 27 (2 + 7 = 9)$ etc.

Strategically reducing the demands on the brain in ways like this, helps many dyslexics achieve success. Different children will struggle with different tasks, and show skills in areas which might be unexpected. Parents need to consider the profile of their individual child.

Dyslexic children have weaknesses that they need to overcome. They also have abilities; and there are tactics to employ that will help them achieve success.

2
At home with dyslexia

By observing and understanding your child within the home, struggles with the outside world become clearer. Facing the challenge of achieving harmony within the home paves the way to greater confidence and success.

For a dyslexic child such as Tom, who struggles at school, the home environment is a welcome refuge ... until it comes to homework, reading, decoding a party invitation, writing a thank-you letter, or constructing a shopping list. He can also find hobbies and games frustrating, and then gets angry or dismissive when attempts are made to encourage success in these areas.

Parents can witness these struggles, despair about failings, get depressed about their implications and berate the child to 'do better, work harder – and turn that television off'. If you recognize these scenarios, you are not alone.

This chapter highlights some of the difficulties some dyslexic children and their families face. It then goes on to suggest how harmony and purpose can be established within the family unit, raising the confidence of the child and their ability to succeed. It also offers ways of encouraging other members of the family to provide a low-level network of support.

Dyslexic difficulties faced within the home

It must be very frustrating to see others scanning the TV guide, gaining both information and enjoyment from the exercise. Frustrating too when you miss your favourite programme through an erroneous consultation of the clock ... when interesting pictures or headlines remain unexplained through a lack of reading ability ... when the cereal box is offering a prize that you cannot discover how to win. Your interest level is high, but access is restricted. You must be stupid. Life isn't fair.

No wonder Clare hurls unpleasant abuse at her brother who does everything so well. In return her brother serves back every gibe he can towards his unfriendly, bossy, bad-tempered sister. Clare's parents face frustrations too. How do they handle this 'difficult' child? How do they balance conflicting interests within the home? And wouldn't life be easier if their daughter went eagerly to school?

Samantha's parents are exasperated by their teenage daughter's untidiness. Frequent arguments occur, along with frantic searches for vital possessions, disrupting family concord. Hormonal changes make Samantha react unfavourably to suggestions that she changes her ways, and additional pressure is put upon her from school as her disorganization affects her ability to arrive prepared for different lessons.

Jonathan, like many children, reacts to his parents at home in a manner that might surprise his teachers. Angry, tearful and/or stubborn behaviour is making Jonathan's family dread the fifteen minutes' daily reading input suggested by the school. Could they be over-pressurizing their son? Is reading time competing with a favourite television programme? Or do they suggest doing it when Jonathan is too tired to be reasonably expected to achieve success?

Jonathan claims the books are too boring. This could reflect his dislike of reading, but it is true that his reading difficulties prevent him from enjoying the comics and books that many of his peers access with ease. Few dyslexic children enjoy the luxury of reading for pleasure. For them, it is not a relaxing process, but hard work.

Additional tensions exist between Jonathan and his grandparents, who are forever presenting him with books to stimulate his interest. Jonathan says that these books are boring too – apart from the ones where you have to find hidden characters and their belongings within intricate drawings. He feels no gratitude towards his grandparents for showering him with such gifts.

Tom and his older brother used to play well together. But when they attempt board games, Tom seems unable to partake without cheating, or suddenly disrupting play despite an initial eagerness to participate.

Mark, at four, is beginning to show unfriendly behaviour towards other children when playing football. Enthusiastic but uncoordinated, Mark is often rebuked for rough behaviour, and berated when the ball gets kicked wildly out of play.

Christopher shows very little interest in football. He loves computer games and making things with his hands but shies away from anything interactive with other people. At home, he is a happy and contented child, quite indifferent to his mathematical difficulties, despite adult concerns being expressed both at home and at school. It is this laid-back attitude that troubles his parents, although their friends suggest that Christopher's placid, good-natured temperament should be valued.

Christopher's parents are confused by their son's lack of reaction to his difficulties; Tom's parents are perplexed by his overreactions. Tom's explosive nature is prompted by reading or numerical challenges; Christopher's calm placidity when tackling extra maths with his father is noticeably causing his parents concern.

Supporting dyslexic difficulties within the home

At home, the effects of dyslexia may be subtle; but when disorganization, confusions with the clock, homework, reading and written difficulties impinge upon the ability to partake and succeed, the everyday lives of dyslexic children (and their families) become littered with frustrations and failure.

Dyslexic children need relevant support if they are going to be able to face their difficulties with confidence. They need a sympathetic ear from someone who will listen to their frustrations, and a helping hand to reduce the impact of obstacles.

Poor organizational skills

Poor organizational skills are a feature of many dyslexics. They misplace and forget belongings, instructions and lists; adding to the challenge of everyday life and putting pressure on those around them too.

Helping the child keep their belongings in order, assigning specific places for objects, and looking for alternative solutions to problems will all help to reduce potential areas of stress and conflict. These early lessons will help the dyslexic child take charge of their environment whenever possible, adapting it to their needs rather than always being the one who feels left out.

To relieve some of the frustrations occurring on school-day mornings, a colour-coded school timetable can be placed on Clare's bedroom wall. Buckled shoes (and slip-on plimsolls) remove her struggle with laces, and her school bag packed the previous evening avoids last-minute panics and confrontations. By beginning the day at a calmer pace, Clare is better equipped to settle at school and tackle the day ahead.

Utilizing supportive aids

Holding together the organization of Clare's everyday life is the clock. Clare, like many dyslexics, treats the clock as an alien, incomprehensible object. But by mastering the skill of telling the time, she can gain access to the benefits and independence the clock can bring. But decoding the clock will be difficult for her. Only after a consolidated effort by the family to implement 'little and often' telling-the-time exercises, will Clare really be able to manipulate timekeeping devices with confidence.

These days, clocks and watches may be either digital – using numbers only, such as 17:40 – or analog – showing the time by means of hands. The same time of day can be correctly expressed in several different ways: 17:40 is also 'twenty to six' and 'five forty'. The same span of time is called both 'fifteen minutes' and a 'quarter of an hour'. So, not only can the display of time be confusing, but also the language we use to describe the passage of time – a language understood only by those privy to its complicated code.

Clare needs to *understand* what is being represented by the various clocks around her home; on the video recorder, the microwave oven, the hall clock and her father's watch. Once Clare understands what the hands and liquid crystal displays (LCDs) represent, she too can tell the time and begin to familiarize herself with the judgement of time intervals (for example, noticing how long ten minutes or two hours actually is), synchronizing herself with the people and events in her life.

If you find it difficult teaching your child how to tell the time, refer to the section on 'Telling the time' in Chapter 11.

Many families use a calendar to plot the outline and variations of their daily routines. It warns of forthcoming events, relieves demands on the memory and exposes interesting numerical patterns associated with the number seven. Dyslexic members of the family must not be excluded from access to information other people take for granted. (When Tom reads on the calendar that 'school stops' on Thursday, he whoops with delight. As the entry actually reads 'school sports', elation, for him, is short-lived.)

Be aware of the ways in which you plan and organize your day, and access your child to similar methods of organization. The television guide, a map, the bus timetable – all help towards independent participation, and allow activities to be planned in advance. But with decoding difficulties and inexperience, the dyslexic child may be unable to recognize their value without your support. The cereal packet, the newspaper headlines, and the postcard from George are also sources of knowledge and interest, enticing the reluctant reader into their text. There is also a point where information needs to be *given*. Show your child that, usually, requests for help can be made and answered with ease. Otherwise, the child may stop asking questions to avoid the demands that are often put upon them before the answer to their query is revealed.

Computers are used by many families for entertainment. Keyboard skills, decision-making and accuracy are required to open the doors to computer literacy and technological knowledge. These may take the dyslexic child longer to learn, but instant feedback is rewarding. Spell-checkers (for the older child), neatly printed displays and ease of correction are advantages that come with word processing software. For those unable to access the written word, synthesized speech will translate material off the screen.

If your child has access to computer equipment at home, encourage them to use it and become familiar with its control. Technology offers many solutions to those able to access its use.

Useful hobbies

Clare's interest in stamp collecting can help her to develop reading skills as well as widen her knowledge of the world. At present, the whole task is beyond her, but by looking carefully at the component parts of her hobby (the stamps, their values, their origin, the album layout itself) separately, these aspects can then be rewardingly combined with success. With other members of the family adding their support through help with pronunciations and identification of names and symbols, Clare's difficulties will become better understood and appreciated by those around her.

Stamp collecting can be very educational, especially for a child who needs to *overlearn* new terminology before it becomes established in their long-term memory. Use a globe to display the world, and practise locating countries. Or locate a country and compare its name with the symbolic information present on stamps. As Clare has a weakness remembering *visual* details, abbreviations will be hard for her. Jonathan will remember an abbreviation, but find it harder pronouncing the terminology it represents.

Other hobbies that utilize literacy include gardening, collecting tea cards, sporting interests and caring for pets. By sharing the experience of consulting books, decoding words and extracting meanings, the child can see the purpose of literacy skills. Without the pressures of a school approach, reading at home can become a shared experience of extracting meaning, achieved without pressure. It will embellish a child's understanding of and involvement in the world about them.

Tom expresses an interest in having a pen pal, until he starts to write a letter. There is nothing wrong with suggesting a child dictates their ideas for you to spell, reducing simultaneous demands on their working memory. Clare has an idea that others may copy: finding a 'tape pal' instead.

After jotting down key words to pace her recording, Clare can express herself with a tape recorder in ways letter-writing would not allow her. It allows her to pause the tape if a major word-finding difficulty presents itself, and removes the challenge of translating speech into the written word. The fact that she has to concentrate hard when listening to her tape pal's reply means Clare's audio skills are exercised too. Her younger brother also asking for a tape pal is an added bonus, raising Clare's self-esteem and allowing her the opportunity to demonstrate expertise to her brother.

A tape recorder is also useful for practising spellings, tables and foreign languages, particularly if the child's own voice is used to make the recordings. Through pre-recorded tapes, the child can access stories they might otherwise miss, perhaps following the words in an accompanying book if one is available. A recorded thank-you message in return for a birthday present is a rewarding alternative to the written word. Again, it uses an alternative approach rather than struggling to achieve a difficult one.

Tape recorders, typewriters and word processors can be presented as 'executive toys' and used to develop further aspects of a hobby or pastime. They can also have useful applications when it comes to homework.

Supporting homework

Parents often ask how, when and if they should support homework tasks set by school. To answer these questions, it is necessary to consider the homework activities from the teacher's point of view. What exactly is the purpose of the exercise in hand?

Having identified the task(s), any additional challenges can be removed. For example, if Clare is required to draw and describe a bedroom of her choice, her teacher would rather you acted as her scribe (removing the spelling element of the activity), than Clare only produce one paragraph of undemanding description due to her lack of confidence and ability to spell more interesting words. If you inform the teacher(s) beforehand of your ability to provide such support, your child need not be excluded from tasks containing a complex reading or written component.

If a child cannot achieve a homework activity through lack of understanding, do inform the school. Many parents, like Christopher's father, provide extra tuition at home, but remember, if your child has not understood a classroom explanation, a different teaching approach may be required. Actual materials for maths, acting out a poem under study, enjoying home-made experiments that illustrate science (floating, sinking, volume, weight, gravity, etc.), may help them to understand concepts more clearly, overlearning new terminology and giving the child the opportunity to discover interesting concepts for itself.

Reading, spelling and maths activities are discussed in the following chapters, as are suggestions for interactive games that develop social skills.

Clumsiness and rough and inappropriate behaviour

A number of dyslexic children – like Mark aged four – behave in a manner that suggests their bodies rather than their eyes, ears or memory are the source of their difficulties. Some seem unaware of body language, so miss subtle messages; others appear to lack awareness of where peripheral parts of their bodies are in relation to the world around them. They are constantly tripping, falling and knocking over things.

There is a condition known as 'dyspraxia' which concerns the neurological development of touch, sound and balance. If your child is exceptionally accident-prone, dislikes the motions of swings and roundabouts, or stands too close to others when interacting with them, then they are exhibiting some of the characteristics of dyspraxia. Dyslexia and dyspraxia can be identified separately, but many dyspraxics are dyslexic too. If you suspect dyspraxia, do investigate this condition further in order to support your child's own individual needs (see Useful addresses).

Explaining their difficulties to a dyslexic child

As you become more aware of the specific needs of your child, you are better equipped to reduce *their* confusions about the struggles they face. How you handle these explanations depends upon the nature and age of your child . . . but it needs to be done. Difficulties need to be recognized and faced; if only so that the child can begin to understand itself as an individual, and not harbour secret worries about some deeper reasons for a failure to succeed.

As Tom discovers his friends are working ahead of him, getting better marks and more favourable opportunities due to their increased literacy skills, Tom gets angry, confused and distressed about school. When his parents explain the cause of his difficulties, Tom is not delighted. But he now knows that his difficulty with spelling is not due to an alien nightmare that he often had in which his brain was replaced with mashed potato. In fact, since his parents and school have begun helping him more with reading and writing, Tom has stopped having that nightmare. Finding out that Uncle Joe couldn't spell either was reassuring. Being allowed story tapes out of the library every week; having a new watch with an easy-to-fasten strap; and making Granny a pop-up card instead of writing a letter are all recent changes that have made life for Tom a little easier.

As the child begins to feel that those around them are sympathetic to their needs (in an understanding, not over-demanding manner), confidence in themselves and others can develop, helping to reduce insecurity, confusion and distress.

The supportive role of grandparents and siblings

Within the home, family members interact together with varying degrees of harmony. When one family member – for whatever reason – is treated or responds differently to situations occurring within the home, conflict or confusions can occur. Siblings do need to be made aware of the specific needs of a dyslexic brother or sister, just as they would be informed of any other factor that affects the life of one of the family members. Detailed explanations are not necessary, but 'house rules' that ban the mockery of weak spelling, reading or numerical skills highlight those areas of life the dyslexic finds difficult. 'We cannot all be good at everything' is a valuable maxim to quote – ideally supported with examples of the dyslexic's achievements in other skills such as swimming, drawing or singing. We are all different, finding some things easy and other things difficult. While the dyslexic child needs to understand that teasing commonly takes place between children, and that remarks should not be taken too seriously, brothers and sisters also need to appreciate how upsetting insensitive remarks can be.

Discussing your child's dyslexia with others is a good idea, but the child can feel embarrassed and ridiculed if conversations are not conducted with sensitivity. Nobody wants to hear their failings aired or have their achievements belittled through insensitive comparisons. But unless you familiarize others with the specific needs of your child, they will be unable to help. They usually do want to help, and by keeping them informed you reduce the occurrence of unintentional mistakes so easily made by those unfamiliar with specific 'hidden' difficulties. Simple pointers, such as asking for clear penmanship in letters or providing suitable ideas for gifts, encourage relations to be supportive.

Individual difficulties

Christopher's difficulties centre around mathematics. At eight years old, he has achieved a reading age of eight years one month, and a spelling age of seven years nine months, so he is just achieving success in these areas. But in matters of numeracy, he remains well behind his peers.

Mathematics uses a symbolic code to represent number and operational instructions. Christopher is confused about this symbolic code, partly because the adults around him assume he has a basic understanding of the notation involved. They tend to chide him rather than uncover and rectify the source of his misunderstandings. Christopher has not yet confidently grasped the difference between '7' and '70', 'a third' and 'the third', the letter 'P' and the number '9'. Not only are some individual digits, such as 7, reversed, but also his numbers: '18' becomes '81'.

Christopher is also often confused by the varied terminology used in class instructing the children what to do: 'add' and 'plus'; 'lots of' and 'multiplied by'; 'take away' and 'subtraction'. Even when the symbols are written down, a confusion remains about which symbol represents which operational instruction, and in which direction sequences of events should go.

To reduce Christopher's confusion, he needs to be taken back to basics and helped to understand the structure of the numerical world. Very slowly and with plenty of material support (in the way of building bricks, dried peas and drinking straws), numbers and sums need to be explained, discovered and understood before the child's confidence in his ability is reduced any further. Many dyslexics have to work very hard to manipulate the symbols of numeracy. They need achievable practice to ensure basic principles are understood, so they can then combine symbols together to depict the language and purpose of mathematics.

There are many ways you can help a child who is having problems with numeracy, particularly once you have identified the source(s) of *their* difficulties.

The numbers 2, 3 and 7 are often reversed. (Draw a picture of a swan swimming towards the left, in the top right-hand corner of a page. This picture is easier for the dyslexic child to remember than a symbol. The movement involved when stroking across the swan's head and down its back mimics the initial shape of the 2, 3 and nearly the 7 . . . enough to reduce reversals.) By attaching an appropriate story to a symbol, the memory can be prompted to provide the correct formation of the letter or number. For example, '9' can be correctly drawn if the symbol 'c' is executed before the stick (preventing the letter 'P' appearing instead). To encourage the production of this 'c', Christopher's teacher has told him the theory of cats having nine lives – connecting the number '9' with the letter 'c'. By repeating this memory jolter, Christopher is now able to produce the number '9' with ease.

As everyone increases their ability to provide a low-profile level of support, the dyslexic child becomes less anxious about their difficulties, and more confident about asking for help. Relationships within the home can then become less fraught, united by a caring, sharing approach to the challenges of life.

3

Reading matters

Before we can read its language, the code of the written word must be cracked.

Difficulties with reading are usually one of the first indications to parents of a child's dyslexia. In retrospect, they can often identify earlier signs of their child's specific learning difficulty; but when the reading books come home from school, and confusions with the printed word persist, parents face the realization that everything is not going smoothly.

The ability to read depends on both teaching and learning skills. This chapter looks at weaknesses within the profile of the dyslexic child that hamper their reading skills, and illustrates supportive teaching methods that help to address the frustrations and failures experienced by dyslexics.

Dyslexic children are not the only ones to find reading difficult. Illness, stress or lack of maturity can affect the acquisition of literacy, and novice readers will experience failures purely due to the complexity of the English language and the arrival of words whose meanings are, as yet, unknown to them.

Keep records of your child's reading achievements and failures, and keep the school informed of the developmental progress of your child.

Tom has been finding reading meaningless, tiring and confusing. Difficulties within his visual memory make it hard for him to recognize whole-word patterns. Although he attempts to break words down into sounds, his poor symbol-to-sound manipulation means this decoding route is ineffective too. However, Tom has discovered a way of reading unknown words which brings him a bit more success: contextual guesswork. By extracting all the clues he can from the surrounding text and pictures, he then guesses at an unknown word. This is not a bad tactic, but it is extremely ineffective without the backup of other decoding processes. He cannot deduce enough words to establish an accurate thread of meaning. Occasionally, Tom's guesses are correct, which confuses his parents. How can he read 'ambulance' on one page, yet struggle with 'away' on the next?

In order to help your child improve their reading, you will need to help them discover the variety of approaches they can use in order to decode an unknown word. And then, without a doubt, the route to better reading is through achievable practice, and the rewarding discovery that books contain interesting and exciting material that is worth decoding for.

There are three ways a written word can be decoded into its spoken form:

1 Break the word down into sound bites corresponding to letter-groups: sh-ip, ra-tion, ex-er-cise. Then blend the parts together.
2 Whole-word memory – matching words with previously stored memory traces: 'said', 'new', 'Europe'. The word is recognized as a whole unit.
3 Contextual guesswork: suggesting a word that fits the sense of the text.

The practised reader fluctuates between these different approaches, depending on the nature of the word under scrutiny and the type of text surrounding it.

Once a reader has established the sound-to-letter-groups, these can be accessed from the memory. When a reader becomes familiar with a whole word, it too is stored in the memory to be used as a template when the same word, or a similar version of the word, is met.

The meanings of words are remembered so that we can understand what we are reading, and are prepared for the coming text. If surrounding text is complicated, a sentence may have to be reread before it is understood.

'Normal' readers increase the number of words in their memory traces with ease. Dyslexic readers struggle. That is why we need to support their reading and writing efforts.

As you can see, reading involves memory processes, the interaction of different decoding methods and purpose. If any of these factors is lacking, success will be limited, increasing the reader's reluctance to continue.

Tom has a number of crucial weaknesses that need supporting before his reluctance will disappear. He needs rewarding inputs that will build up his knowledge of sound-to-letter-group relationships, and single-word reading games that will increase his whole-word vocabulary. He also needs to share the experience of reading with others who will support his ability to extract meaning from the text. Equipped with a better understanding of words, and more effective decoding approaches, Tom's enthusiasm can be rekindled again as he begins to find success. Tom can, and should, be using guesswork, but only after the odds of guessing wrongly have been reduced.

Identifying reading weaknesses

In order to increase your child's ability to read, consider these questions:

How does *your* child tackle an unknown word? Sound it out . . . t-r-i-u-m-p-h? Guess at it by its overall shape . . . trump? Or guess at it by considering the meaning of surrounding words . . . victory?

Does your child *consistently* avoid one of the three decoding methods – of the breakdown and blending of sound-to-letter-groups; of whole-word recognition, and of guesswork?

How long will a new word be remembered for? A page of reading? A day? A week? (This will vary, but it gives you some idea of their memory skills. It also tells you how frequently learning inputs need to be delivered (see Chapter 9, 'Memory matters').

Does your child read a 'little and often' every day? If not, ideally they should. Ten minutes after tea each day is better than an hour on Sundays, and allows a variety of different material to be experienced (for example, the TV guide, poetry, an instruction manual, a short story, a letter from a friend, comparison of shampoo bottle labels).

Is there a topic of type of reading your child particularly likes? It might be comics, ghost stories, children's adventures, animal stories, true stories.

When you have a rough idea of your child's decoding weaknesses and strengths, and have secured some written material that you know will be of interest to them (story book, newspaper article, joke book, historical play), 'shared reading' can become a *successful* experience for you both.

Reading successfully together

'Shared reading' describes activities that provide learning support to the reader in order that they can achieve success. Here are a few examples:

- Read aloud 'together', your voice carrying the meaning forward, dropping back if the child meets an achievable word, taking over if a difficulty is faced. Use your finger to direct the eyes smoothly from left to right.
- You read a page, the child repeats it. Again, use your finger; pausing it if mistakes are made, perhaps pointing to specific parts of a word to be noticed.
- The child reads a page in their head, then answers questions you put to them. (You may find that meaning can be more effectively extracted when the demand to read aloud is removed.) Select individual words, discuss their make-up, meaning and pronunciation. Then read the piece aloud together.
- Scan a page quietly together, taking it in turns to select a word to 'take apart', looking at its meaning, spelling and pronunciation. Then, each make a guess at the storyline from the few words selected before reading it through.
- Find a play, write a play, or assign yourselves to the different characters in a book. Make it more fun by adopting silly voices, and relieve the pressure by silently reading through your speeches first.

English words can be roughly divided into two types: those that follow sound-to-symbol spelling 'rules' (for example, home, Rome), and those that do not (for example, come, some). The latter need to be accessed from the whole-word sight vocabulary. The former can be decoded through sounds, and then stored in the whole-word sight vocabulary once they become familiar. (See also Chapter 4, 'Spelling issues'.)

When you come across an unknown word in the text you are reading, your choice of decoding approach largely depends on the word under scrutiny. Point out its peculiarities, match it with similarly spelled words, hunt out smaller words or familiar word-chunks within the word – anything to get it noticed. It is often better to 'give' a word during reading, to prevent the meaning of the text from being lost. Then go back to the word and discuss it after the passage is finished.

Breaking words into chunks is a necessary process when decoding words, for a number of reasons. It helps to access the meaning of words (for example, un-tied). It reduces the memory load (for example, some-thing). It highlights spelling patterns (for example, n-ight-ly), and it transforms a daunting word into achievable units (for example, ex-plo-sive).

Explaining the meanings of words is vital. This is an exercise that gives the opportunity for you to practise thesaurus skills where words with similar meanings are listed: huge, big, gigantic, etc. This is a useful tactic for any poor speller: when not sure how to spell 'pause', use 'wait' instead. (But do not suggest this tactic too early, or the child may avoid using interesting vocabulary through their lack of spelling ability.)

As you read through books together, and gain meaning and purpose from the words, look too at the writing *style*. Notice how some sentences are short. Others are long and descriptive as the author attempts to portray their characters and situations in expressive language: 'the thin, smelly black cat' is more distinctive than 'the cat'. Normally, the dyslexic has not the ability or inclination to observe such details. The decoding business saps them dry. But, as they are also writers themselves, they need to know that not only are descriptive passages more interesting to read, but that the display of words expresses a wealth of meaning.

Remember though, your primary task is to access your child to the printed word through achievable, interesting and worthwhile reading practice. Teachers do not have as much time as they would like for one-to-one reading sessions and can rarely curl up on the sofa for ten minutes to investigate a new library book with an individual child. Even busy parents can manage that. And sharing the experience keeps the parents informed of their child's personal achievements, interests and goals.

Additional factors that reduce reading proficiency

Clare's eyesight and ocular muscle proficiency have been tested, but nothing has been found to explain her specific difficulties with reading. For some children, wearing spectacles is recommended. The lenses may be tinted, or prescribed to strengthen weaknesses in the focusing and tracking elements of sight. If prescribed correctly, these can result in a significantly improved ability to tackle the printed word. Due to the variety of specific learning difficulties, solutions for one child will not always work for another; but it is worth talking to other parents if only to discover what options are available for investigation.

Through a mixture of optical difficulties, a straightforward sentence can become a complete muddle. For example, 'The dog ran across the road' may be perceived as, 'Thed og rana acrossac ross ther oad.' Rearranged sequences and guesswork can result in mistakes. For example, 'She was ready for the party' may be read as, 'She saw danny from the party.'

The English language is full of homophones (words that sound the same but are spelled differently). Saw/sore, threw/through are examples. To access the individual meaning of these words, the reader has to decode the word using a variety of information stored in their memories. Any weaknesses in these channels will lead to possible misunderstanding. A book that contains too many challenges is too frustrating to be enjoyed; so the reader is likely to lack understanding, motivation and success.

'I'm too tired to read,' complains Jonathan after a long day at school. He probably is, so the timing of his reading input needs to be considered carefully. A rest after school is fine before homework demands are met. It usually helps to designate a regular time for working – straight after tea or at 6 p.m. – anything to remove the opportunity for disruptive bargaining attempts at postponing the inevitable. As Jonathan finds his fifteen-minute reading practice is unavoidable, and success in it becomes achievable with a parent's help, so his hostility subsides, increasing still further his ability to succeed. However, dramatic reading improvements do not occur overnight. Success is slow and irregular, still leaving the child excluded from access to many of the books enjoyed by their peers. It is therefore important to keep home-reading exercises separate from 'the bedtime story'. This is another experience altogether, and a vital input for the child who cannot extract meaning from reading material on their own.

Access to reading

The bedtime story can be provided by story tapes, with or without an accompanying book. Or they can be presented 'live', shared and enjoyed together – living proof that reading is an enjoyable and very useful skill. You can give your child a way into the books their peers are reading, and share with them articles or stories that add to an interest, hobby or topic at school.

Stories and information can also be found in comics and magazines aimed at children. The use of capital letters in some of the comics is not a problem; the content of some of the magazines might be! But anything that interests a struggling reader has to be worth investigating, familiarizing the child with the format and content of short, self-contained written pieces.

Samantha has gained a lot from the young-teenager magazines that she reads. And Tom, once helped with initial decoding, will reread a comic a number of times for enjoyment, perceiving the stories as 'fun' rather than 'boring' like the longer ones written in books.

Building up reading confidence

Even as dyslexic readers get older and more proficient, they will often still baulk when faced with a page packed with words, so use a piece of *plain* card to block some of it from view. Also, point out how the interest level of the storyline can be increased with more words. 'The elephant escapes' *or* 'The homesick young elephant shook his chain all night. In the morning, one of his captors took away the chain and tied him up with a rope instead. "Ha!" thought the elephant, "I can chew through that in no time. Goodbye, you smelly lumberjacks . . .".'

Samantha, at thirteen, may find books within the large-print section of the library attract her interest and are easier to read than the small-print-blurring-to-the-eyes text of the teenage section. Letters from friends provide short, interesting messages for her to read, and membership of an ornithology club supplies her with a colourful, reader-friendly magazine each month, complete with competitions and puzzles that she likes to enter – practising a number of literacy skills.

Single-word reading games will increase the child's ability to recognize individual words, and discriminate between visually similar ones. Games that put together the syllable components of words will also boost reading, helping to familiarize the child with the breaking down and building up of sound bites to produce meaning. Matching together words that are connected (bucket, spade); or opposites (black, white); or are commonly found together (getting, ready), support reading because they stimulate contextual prompting (preparing the brain to expect forthcoming words).

As reading skills improve, confidence grows. Keep widening your child's exposure to reading, but try not to stretch it ahead too quickly. Achievable success promotes overlearning and strengthens earlier lessons, allowing gradual extension when the reader is willing and able.

Street names, shop signs, advertisements, labels, posters, instructions, items for sale – the written word is all around us. Practise reading it wherever you go.

4
Spelling issues

Words are meaningful, but that meaning remains inaccessible until the code of the symbolic language of letters is understood.

This chapter considers the spelling and writing difficulties caused by dyslexia. Many children 'pick up' spellings with ease, but the dyslexic child is often unable to absorb the details of the written code in the 'traditional' way. They need to have spellings explained to them, and then these spellings must be used and learnt through teaching inputs that will bring them success.

By considering individual spelling errors (have a look through a sample of school exercise books), weaknesses in the dyslexic's spelling profile can be identified, along with their strengths. By understanding the principles behind spelling lore, remedial support can be structured to suit the individual's needs, incorporating games and adaptable exercises to practise valuable lessons.

Hampering the ability to manipulate the sounds and shapes of symbolic representations of words, dyslexia will naturally impede an individual's ability to spell. They may also have difficulties handling a pen, forming individual letters and presenting their written work neatly.

Clare, our struggling philatelist, is becoming more familiar with the abbreviations and symbols adopted by different nations and the protocol that allows British stamps merely to display the Queen's head. However, when Clare attempts to write down the names of the countries that produce the best stamps, she makes numerous errors. Clare may now be able to 'recognize' a country's name, or the symbols associated with it, but she cannot recall the details of its spelling. This leads her to rely on a *phonological* approach when reproducing many words. So she produces, for example, Ingland, Jermuny, Ostreea.

Jonathan, on the other hand, reproduces words through their *visual* components, not their sounds. 'Germany' might become 'Germoy', and 'Austria' be spelled 'Astia'.

A whole-word approach to spelling

The whole-word assimilation of unknown words is not unusual. Quite often, even proficient readers meet an unfamiliar word (usually a name), in a book and classify it in their minds only as 'S – long word, the girl with the blond hair', or 'Th . . . ski; that Polish place where B . . . th . . . ri went to school'. Ask the reader to articulate or write the name, and they can find it impossible. Because they did not dissect the word into its component sounds (entering the word into their verbal vocabulary), or did not study the sequential form of its letters (entering it fully into their visual vocabulary), the details of the word remain a blur. Moreover, if the word is foreign, spelling and pronunciation errors may be made due to an unfamiliarity with the different sound-to-symbol spelling rules involved. These are the types of difficulty faced by the dyslexic child all the time.

A *phonological spelling approach*

Dissecting written words into sounds requires some knowledge of the letter-to-sound relationships and rules. Because of varied cultural and foreign influences over the years, the English language has many different spelling rules, and plenty of riddles too. These have to be understood, memorized and recognized if the ability to translate words into their written form is going to be achieved. With only 26 letters and many, many different phonemes (chunks of sound) to reproduce, surely it is more amazing that most children acquire spelling proficiency with the ease that they do, than surprising when a few of them do not!

Identifying spelling weaknesses through errors

Tom is losing all desire to commit pen to paper. His verbal vocabulary is good, but his written work is constantly marked by poor spellings, untidy corrections and indeterminate letter shapes halfway between an 'a' and an 'o', a 'g' or a 'y'. Tom tries to 'sound words out' when he spells, as can be seen by his typical errors:

said/sed, was/wos, want/wont, told/towd, called/cord, money/muny, teacher/teecher, football/ftborl

Jonathan's spelling errors are equally informative. His whole-word

29

approach and sequencing difficulties can be seen by errors such as:

market/manhet, pushed/puhsed, beginning/beggining, fought/
forgut, light/lught, king/gnil (reversed impression)

By looking through school exercise books, a wide range of spelling
errors can be used to assess the nature of an individual's spelling
difficulties. You can also witness progression over time, finding which
words are reliably entered into the child's spelling vocabulary, and
which mistakes have become established errors rather than occasional
'hiccups'.

Understanding spelling

It helps parents to understand how and why some words are spelled
because very often, a word is written down without a second's thought
for the phonetical or physical characteristics that have just been
displayed. But the dyslexic child will need the mechanics of written
language to be explained in more detail. As they have failed to pick up
spelling patterns through normal teaching methods, alternative methods of teaching and learning are required to 'crack' the spelling code –
taught to them in a way that *they* can learn.

The history of English spelling makes interesting reading and, for
the older child, includes factors that reinforce history lessons at school.
For example, a large number of Dutch workers came to England when
the Industrial Revolution provided them with opportunities for work.
Many joined the printing presses, which meant some English words
acquired unusual lettering due to the influence of the Dutch tongue.
Words like 'night' and 'fight' are thought to have gained the 'igh'
pattern this way.

Once dictionaries became popular, words that had previously been
spelled only according to the abilities of the writer, became established
according to decisions made by the books' compilers. As spoken
language changed over the years, spellings stood (almost) still, which
can make the matching of some spellings to their modern pronunciation extremely difficult, often impossible. For example, the silent 'k' in
words such as 'knight' and 'knave' were pronounced in the seven-
teenth century. The 'h' of 'hour' and 'honest' were never intended to
be pronounced, because of the rules of Latin, but 'hospital' and
'humour' have become Anglicized over time.

Spellings can be loosely categorized into two groups. The first group contains words whose spellings match (through familiar sound-to-letter-group rules) the sound of the word that is spoken.

car, sight, church, letter, black, swimming

Words that contain recognized spelling patterns can usually be grouped with other words following similar spelling rules:

round	hat	hate	got	goat
sound	mat	mate	cot	coat
ground	fat	fate	hot	soak

- note the vowel sounds;
- vowels crucially affect pronunciation and spellings;
- vowels affect each other.

Words that share a spelling pattern and similar *sound* (for example, laid, aid, stain) can be collected and used to play games. Use words that are useful to *your* child, extending the list as their confidence and ability grows. Always introduce the *meaning* and likely *context* of a word with its spelling – utilizing spoken, printed and written examples.

Clare will find it easy to group together words that share a common element of sound because her audio memory is good. But when she has to choose between the spelling of 'goat' or 'gote', her *visual* memory will be called into play too. So, when introducing a family of words that share a spelling pattern: use colour to highlight similarities; point out familiar letter-patterns within the words; and try to connect words together (for example, n*augh*ty d*augh*ter and th*ough*tfully b*ough*t).

The other group of spellings is the 'odd bods'. These are words whose spellings do not match modern pronunciation, and spellings that don't follow the rules. The words 'was, want, their, debt, grass (when pronounced gr-ar-s), hour, friend, because, said' are all odd bods. A word ending in '-tion' might also be considered as an odd bod by the child not yet familiar with the -tion spelling pattern.

Jonathan will like odd bods, and will learn them quite easily. Their lack of symbol-to-sound regularity and their need to be assimilated into the visual memory will suit his learning style.

Clare, whose visual modality is poor, may be helped by the deliberate mispronunciation of words during the learning process in order that they then trigger her audio memory instead. For example, 'friend' becomes 'fri-end', 'knife' becomes 'k-nife', and 'calendar' can be oddly pronounced (when spelling), to emphasize its '-ar' ending.

Odd bods need to be recognized as 'odd' and learnt apart from their 'regular' relations. A memory 'tab' can be incorporated to highlight eccentric spellings.

It is impossible to spell 'impossible' without two 'i's.
It is necessary to wear one collar and two socks (1 'c', 2 's's).
Big Elephants Can Always Understand Small Elephants ...
BECAUSE they speak the same language.
'said' – Sally Anne Is Dead (dramatic, but effective).

Learning spelling through play

'Play' doesn't necessarily mean 'easy', but it does mean *fun*. Cover a steamed-up window with words describing a farmyard, write in sand a list of words that share a spelling pattern, and play word games that help to develop spelling proficiency.

By adding a competitive and/or humorous element to the task of learning spellings, players want to learn, achieve and win. Games allow the 'manipulation' of letters and words. A penny can drop or a memory trace can be created for life as the playing of the game allows the sound and sequential details, letter-bonds and meanings to be manoeuvred and understood.

The following games are short and adaptable. Play them anywhere, with anyone, adding to them your own and your child's ideas.

Six games to establish occurrence of a sound-to-letter-group

Collect about 20 words that match your child's vocabulary require-ments. Keep to words that share the target sound-to-letter-group. For the purposes of demonstration, suppose the group is 'ir'. Choose words that include the 'bird' sound, not just the occurrence of 'i' followed by 'r' – for example, do *not* use 'mirror'. Make a neat, clear master-list of words with each 'ir' written in red, highlighting its presence and its association with its sound in these words. Also copy these words onto cards large enough to handle, but without highlighting the 'ir' pattern. Add and remove cards as ability and confidence grows.

third, bird, ladybird, girl, twirl, schoolgirl, skirt, shirt, dirt, birthday, birth, rebirth, girth, girder, thirsty, thirty, dirty, fir, sir, stir, stirring, stirred, first, third, thirst, skirting, circle, circled, circumference, circuits, circulation

1. Match the endings
Youngest begins. Shuffle cards, deal four to each player. Place remaining pack face-down on the table. First player takes a card off the pack. *If* they have two words in their hand whose *last two, three or four letters* are identical, they place them on the table, and read them out. The winner is the one who collects the most pairs of words.

2. Read 'em off your chest
Player takes deep breath. How many words off the master-list or the cards can be correctly read aloud before the breath runs out? Improved performances score points.

3. Matching lengths
Oldest begins (calculate ages). Same play as for Match the endings. This time words of the same *length* are collected into pairs. Extend the list of words by adding suffixes and prefixes, making plurals, etc.

4. Pelmanism
Make duplicate cards for *some* of the words on your list, adding pairs of plurals and other lengthened words to add variety. Shuffle, then lay out the cards face down on the table. Players take it in turns to attempt to uncover pairs of identical words. This is a good memory game, adaptable for many purposes.

5. Absent friends
Erase/obscure two, three or four letters of each word. Player has to fill in the missing letters correctly or undergo a fun penalty (run around the table backwards reciting the spelling of the word – you can make mistakes too).

6. *Key words*

As cards are turned over, each player *speaks* a sentence that illustrates the use of that word. Every sentence must be different from another already spoken – how different is up to you. Include sentences you might find in a newspaper, on TV, in a fairy tale or instruction booklet. For the next round, each player *writes* a sentence for each word, scoring a point for every word that is *unique* among other players' contributions, plus three points if the 'key' word is spelled correctly.

Spelling lessons

When discovering new spellings, it is paramount that the child is encouraged to 'chunk' words into smaller parts. Not only can the memory handle these smaller units more successfully, and the meaning of the word be more clearly understood (for example, un-kind), but the procedure mimics one of the decoding processes used in reading. Overlapping spelling and reading procedures helps to establish the relationship between coding and decoding words. Matching spelling-sounds with their component letters (for example, sh-op), encourages the same type of chunking when decoding an unknown word in a reading book.

As Jonathan becomes familiar with common words (see Chapter 11, 'Activities'), and with common suffixing and prefixing rules, he will become more confident and willing to reproduce his ideas on paper. By perfecting frequently encountered words, the percentage of errors is reduced, improving the look of written work as well as boosting the writer's confidence. As Jonathan also becomes familiar with high-frequency letter groupings ('ir', 'er', 'ai' 'oo', etc.), he will be helped to make better educated guesses when faced with producing an unknown spelling. Jonathan needs to know that misspelling a word is not the end of the world so, if he wants to use a word, he should do so. If he is unsure of a spelling, he should make an educated guess based on the *sounds* within the word, which will increase the ability of his reader to understand what he has written.

Note your child's achievements in a booklet by ticking off successes as the words are used in context or in games. If their tally is good, your child can tick their achievements off themselves on a master-list. When a word has been spelled correctly on three different occasions, cross it off the list and the child can give themselves a pat on the back.

Here are two more activities to adapt in order to incorporate words your child specifically needs to practise.

Daily growth

This writing activity can be played over a period of days. On day one, dictate *two* words which the child writes down with your help (for example, The twenty . . .). On day two, repeat these two words and add two more (for example, The twenty fat tadpoles . . .). Each day the child is repeating past words as the sentence exposes its meaning: The twenty / fat tadpoles / which Matthew / caught yesterday / escaped when / Jennifer pulled / out the / bath plug.

A reluctant child will believe the demands of this activity are very low, and so be willing to participate; yet the value gained by using, recalling, manipulating words on a daily basis is very high. Aspects such as handwriting can be practised too, followed by questions such as 'What is a tadpole?', 'Where do you think the tadpoles will go?' and 'How old do you think Matthew and Jennifer are?'

Another game that can be used for different spellings – perhaps a school spelling list, countries, odd bods, or key words for a new school topic – is:

Dicey spellings

With one dice and words written on cards, player *looks* and *reads aloud* a word (or has the word read to them when their ability grows), then throws the dice. According to the number thrown, and without referring back to the card, the player has to reproduce the spelling

1	spell word aloud, letter by letter	*forwards*
2	spell word aloud, letter by letter	*backwards*
3	write, eyes open	*forwards*
4	write, eyes closed	*forwards*
5	write with opposite hand to normal writing hand	*forwards*
6	throw dice again	

following the instructions below. These incorporate known techniques to enter material into the long-term memory. Let players self-correct their results. Repeat daily until spellings are secure.

Putting spellings into context

Spelling words in isolation is one thing. Writing strings of words that simultaneously convey meaning is another matter. Make sure your child *uses* words they are learning how to spell, and continues to use them regularly.

Children love to make their own books – a diary of a holiday; a day in the life of a goldfish, cat or millionaire; a cartoon collection; a joke book. Children must discover that writing can be *fun*, and that spellings are not the only consideration of the finished piece.

Matching the spelling with the meaning of a word is very important, particularly if the word is a 'homophone'. Homophones are words that 'sound' the same but are spelled differently (for example there/their). Unfortunately, there are a number of common homophones which often cause spelling confusions. By making it a game to see how many homophones *adults* can think of (perhaps around the dinner table or on a car journey), the child is introduced to this concept before you begin to write words down. It is a good idea to write down homophones using colour, pictures and meaningful sentences. If the words are displayed on a wall poster, they can be frequently observed and remarked upon.

Be sensitive about your child's willingness to have spelling lessons displayed for all to see, but the wall by the toilet, the ceiling above their bed and the inside of cupboard doors are all good places to display wall posters of various kinds.

Supporting achievement

By using and learning from the words *your* child finds difficult to spell, they can see the reward of extra lessons. Match familiar words with other words that share visual and audio elements; associate them with words of similar or opposite meaning; and write words whenever you can. But also remember how difficult spelling actually is for the dyslexic child.

With a deep-rooted weakness within the storage and recall processes concerned with the sound-to-symbol code of written speech, dyslexics are unlikely ever to be proficient spellers. Ensure that they can use the resources around them relevant to their needs, such as dictionaries, spell checkers and other people. And frequently ignore all spelling mistakes, centring your attention and comments on the written content instead. Because unless children discover a useful (and achievable) purpose to writing, they will become reluctant to commit their thoughts and ideas to paper, and suffer too from the lack of experience these activities bring.

Penmanship difficulties

Handwriting skills develop over time. Young hands and fingers do not possess the muscular dexterity required to execute fine lettering. Physical and mental maturity, along with teaching input, is required before letters can be correctly and carefully formed.

Dyslexic children often develop fine-motor skills more slowly than their peers. This can lead to poor handwriting attempts, disjointed letters and words scattered irregularly across the page. The situation can be further encumbered if the child is also a left-handed writer – as many dyslexics are.

Poor penmanship further reduces a dyslexic's self-esteem. If something looks good, at least the child can gain credit for that. If, however, there is nothing in appearance, content or spelling worthy of praise, the child quickly loses all incentive to commit their ideas to paper.

To help develop fine-muscular control in the fingers, along with hand-to-eye coordination – play with buttons, paints and puzzles. Practise writing individual letters in sand, on blackboards and in colour, paying particular attention to the beginning and ending point of each letter. Ask your school for two written alphabets (small and capital letters), so that writing practice at home follows the same patterns as are required at school, and discover when cursive (joined-up) script is introduced.

Cursive script may seem harder to perform, but for the dyslexic child it has an added advantage. The process of writing a word as one continuous line (which is what effectively happens when individual letters are joined up), helps the processes involved with memory storage and recall. Not only are the *sound* and *shape* of a word registered by the brain as a word is written, but the mechanical movements involved with the hand and arm also pass through the brain.

Tracing individual letters and words, writing in giant script, using chunky pencils that are easy to grip, will all help the skills of penmanship to develop. As writing progresses, choose individual letters to perfect rather than criticize too many, and look at additional elements – such as even spaces between words, tidy methods of correcting mistakes, and clear punctuation.

Left-handed writers will need to develop a writing style that bears the ink pen in mind. It is easier for all children to establish a good writing posture, pen grip and writing style at an early age, rather than try to change established habits later on. The dyslexic child may need to take on adjustments gradually as their skills mature, allowing for the delayed nature in their muscular developments, and ensuring that they are not expected to produce material beyond their capability.

So, keep the school informed of your child's spelling and writing activities and achievements. And expect performance to be erratic at times due to the complex and confusing nature of written language, and the pressure of other demands being made on the working memory.

5

Mathematical concerns

The patterns and concepts of mathematics are depicted by symbols representing meaning or instruction. Without a basic comprehension of this numerical code, development of further understanding is hard to achieve.

Mathematics is a subject that builds upon basic numeracy skills and notational understanding to explain abstract ideas and concepts concerned with shape, size and organized relationships. Mathematics, like the written word, is highly symbolic, with no true correlation between the squiggles of the code and the meanings that they represent. It is only through tradition that the code has established itself in the way that it has.

Many dyslexic children struggle with maths. This chapter looks at the reasons for some of their difficulties, and considers ways in which parents (and teachers) can encourage success. Unlike the code of written speech where the purpose and nature of a symbol can vary (for example, m*a*t, me*a*t, *A*ndrew, r*a*in), mathematical symbols usually remain static. The number '6' may mean six units, six thousands or six tenths, but it still depicts the value 'six'.

Mathematics builds upon foundations of numerical knowledge. If a child misses or misunderstands these early lessons, further confusions are almost guaranteed. Despite their clarity to you or me, '+' and '×' are not so dissimilar to the dyslexic. 'Lots of kisses' can help the multiplication sign become more distinctive and meaningful, and with the division sign, the dots can be used to represent the sharing out process.

The placement position of numbers is of vital importance to their meaning. So 73 is very different from 37 or 703. Dyslexics may find this difficult as they often lack the dimensional understanding and memory of such symbolic matters, but they can achieve success. It may take them longer than their peers to perfect independence away from labelled columns for the hundreds, tens and units; but unless these notational foundations are secure, further misunderstanding, confusion and failure will occur.

Christopher's parents have discussed their son's difficulties with his class teacher who, in return, has given them details of mathematical topics being covered in school, and discussed ways in which Christopher's specific learning difficulties can be addressed in class. By also showing Christopher's parents the school's preferred layout and procedural methods when tackling sums, Christopher will receive complementary support from home, reinforcing the lessons he is having in class. Christopher's parents also discover that different multiplication tables are being learnt each week (information that Christopher was not bringing home), and that mental arithmetic tests are held every Wednesday morning. Christopher's teacher has noticed that Christopher's number bonding skills are weak. The number bonds of 10 are particularly useful (for example, 7+3, 2+8), but also bonds such as 8+7, 10+4, 9+8, should be learnt so that they produce an almost automatic response, to speed up mathematical performance and reduce calculation mistakes. These take time to learn, require repetitive practice and constant revision (see Chapter 6, 'Educational play').

Another example of numbers bonding together in a familiar way is displayed in multiplication tables. If we can recall, with accuracy, that '$7 \times 6 = 42$', the speed of our calculation is increased, and any errors caused by miscalculating $6+6+6+6+6+6+6 = 42$, is removed. Unfortunately, most dyslexics find multiplication tables desperately difficult to learn reliably enough to provide their memories with an accurate answer when they need it. And even if one of these multiplication bonds is secured, the length of time that it remains accurately accessible to the mind can be very short. Sometimes, the answer is completely forgotten, or, worse still, an erroneous answer is produced which the child mistakenly believes is completely accurate.

Attaching the sequence of multiplication tables to material objects may help – a family of mice for the four times table, octopuses for the eights (see Chapter 11, 'Activities'), but many dyslexic children will also require experience using a tables square and calculator if they are going to achieve long-term success.

Calculators, like keyboards, do not replace learning skills, but they do remove elements which are known to cause difficulties for many dyslexic children. Tom, for example, has very untidy penmanship and his spatial display of work is often bizarre. This can easily lead to mathematical mistakes when numbers are inaccurately displayed, or when operational symbols are incorrectly depicted in his book. Mathematical operations make heavy demands of the brain's working memory. If using a calculator reduces some of the additional demands caused by dyslexia, we are more likely to help the dyslexic achieve success.

Clare enjoys maths, even though her performance speed is slow. Her teacher is familiar with the needs of her pupils with specific learning difficulties, knowing that they often require material support for their sums, that new concepts have to be slowly and carefully introduced, and that methodology and rules need regular revision. At ten years old, counting bricks are usually considered childish, so a box of coloured counters is placed on every table during maths, and frequently used by the teacher to illustrate concepts and examples to pupils.

New terminology is thoroughly explained and identified in mathematical displays. Homework sheets always illustrate the nature of the tasks in hand to reduce failures through misunderstood directions. Clare has also been given extra sheets of repetitive numerical practice to establish her skills, and is encouraged to jot numbers down in the page margin before entering them into a sum to reduce reversals that cause mistakes.

But not every child is happy to sit down after school and tackle extra maths. Parents themselves can often do without the aggravation required to persuade their child to attend to and achieve valuable additional work. Often parents need to develop tactics themselves, and incorporate number practice into games through dice, cards and board games. They may also need to bring in extra tuition from outside the family, but if the child is dyslexic, the tutor will need to be suitably trained and experienced in order to understand a dyslexic's specific needs.

Mark is still young, but early counting practice as he plays with his toys and as he climbs up and down stairs will initially help establish the forward and reversed sequence of numbers between one and ten.

Jonathan has strengths within his visual modality which help him to recognize the patterns and shapes displayed by numbers, geometry and graphs. In turn, this has allowed him to become experienced in handling a variety of data that boosts his enjoyment and eagerness to participate in class. He is also able to perform mental arithmetic with relative ease, which relieves his need always to translate equations into symbolic displays.

Samantha used to make frequent mistakes concerning number size, perhaps omitting a nought or misplacing the decimal point. By noting the consistency of her errors, Samantha's specialist support teacher – whom she now sees in school once a week for an hour – has been able to provide some personalized mathematics tuition. These one-to-one lessons have boosted Samantha's ability and confidence. She now makes fewer 'silly' mistakes, having had her particular difficulties drawn to her attention and supportive measures suggested (such as speaking a number quietly to herself as she writes). This extra tuition has increased her ability to produce accurate work and to gain the necessary success required to encourage an understanding of and interest in maths.

Most dyslexics have some difficulty with mathematics, although many overcome their difficulties through the application of material practice to support the symbolic representations of concepts. They may experience isolated problems with certain areas of maths, finding sequential tasks harder to master (such as the solving of equations where an ordered approach is required), and can sometimes 'see' an answer without being able to explain clearly the route by which they achieved their result.

The parent of the dyslexic child must therefore keep an eye on their child's numerical progress, supporting their need for 'little and often' input, liaising with the school to ensure topics that present difficulty can be overlearned at home and that new terminology is clearly understood.

6
Educational play

Learning through play is nothing new . . . children have been doing it for years.

The family of a dyslexic child may notice that they show a negative approach to games. The child may disrupt a game for no apparent reason, or merely show a reluctance to play a new game, despite it containing their favourite elements of excitement, interaction and challenging fun.

This chapter looks at some of the causes for rejection, and its effect on many aspects of learning that games unknowingly teach. We can then see why games can be more than just fun, and can look at some of the ways that lessons can be manipulated to fit into the style of playful enjoyment.

Games make learning fun through their little and often teaching approach which allows overlearning, reinforces memories and enlightens the mind. And, as play is the opposite of work, your child might even enjoy taking part!

This chapter begins by discussing elements of game-play. Three individual sections follow, illustrating games useful to the dyslexic child: card games, dice games and memory games. All these games can be adapted to suit the needs of your child, and others around them who also want to join in with the fun.

Christopher has numerical difficulties, and is teased by his ten-year-old brother when he makes silly mistakes. Now the brothers rarely play any games that involve dice. Tom is clumsy and flounders in ball games. Embarrassed by previous ball-catching failures, and jeered for his lack of football control, Tom dreads sports activities and is excluded from many playground games too.

Clare, at ten, is surrounded by notes in class, Scrabble, hangman and memory games. She hates them all. She lacks the ability to compete, so withdraws herself, out of reach of possible ridicule.

Jonathan comes from a family who like to play card games and board games, which he enjoys too, but he rarely wins. As he struggles to hide difficulties with reading or numbers, others become tactically more able to manipulate the play to bring them success. Jonathan prefers familiar favourites but his older sister is always introducing new games, and teasing Jonathan's failure to grasp the rules as quickly as their younger seven-year-old sister.

As siblings and peers develop ahead of them, weaknesses in literacy and numerical skills become even more evident and embarrassing to the dyslexic child. And when a child who is desperately struggling to take part and win is faced with failure and ridicule, they usually react, not unexpectedly, with hostile or withdrawn behaviour.

But before we decide to save the self-esteem of dyslexic children and ban all games, it is worth considering the educational, social and pleasurable benefits games can bring.

Dyslexic children particularly can benefit from play. Unachievable tasks are no fun for anyone. However, structured, amusing, rewarding activities – when manipulated to include valuable spelling, reading, numerical and sequencing lessons – provide the repetitive overlearning and unstressful discovery required by dyslexic children.

Arguments between siblings are normal. Give them a new game to learn and before long the finest of families are bickering with their enthusiasm to win. A dyslexic child can quickly lose all interest in the game if pressure is loaded upon their errors, and others are mentally ahead of their play. Two ways of reducing this stress are first, to introduce them to a game carefully, in a relaxed manner, before the others are involved; and second, invoke house rules to minimize inter-play provocation and pressure.

A pack of cards is a wonderful learning tool for the dyslexic. It practises skills the child is often struggling to achieve on their own – for example, distinguishing between a '6' and a '9', matching suit symbols, remembering sequences. Card games practise these skills, helping them improve their abilities through play. When doing a maths sum at school, you do not want to be held up deciding between the '6' and '9' squiggles: this is just the type of difficulty a dyslexic child is likely to face.

Maybe they miss the '5' out when counting; perhaps they initially find the suits hard to identify and name. Becoming proficient with rules is helpful memory experience and the mere handling of cards is good fine-motor muscle exercise.

Good spelling games can be easily made or adapted at home to suit the individual nature of your child's spelling needs. Dyslexic children need the overlearning practice that games provide; they need to see and use spellings and be able to match sounds to letters repeatedly if they are going to establish accurate, long-term memory traces.

Computer programs that combine spelling and reading lessons with fun are available, and can be used to improve a variety of skills along with familiarizing the child with the keyboard – an invaluable advantage as they get older.

Reading can also be practised when playing games. Familiarize the child with text that appears repeatedly in a game, for example, 'move back four spaces'. Encourage them to read the instructions aloud. If the game is frequently played, advanced reading words can be practised before play. Games you have created yourself – perfectly matching reading ability with play – are ideal, for example, home-made trivia questions and treasure hunts (see Chapter 11, 'Activities').

Playing games that use two or more dice helps to establish number bonds (for example, $6 + 6 = 12$), that can then be quickly, and accurately, recalled to aid numerical tasks. Scoring number games can be embarrassingly stressful, but house rules can prevent teasing and ridicule. When totalling scores, the ability to remove oneself from the distraction of anticipating players should be allowed, encouraging the child to practise their addition in peace.

Although the faculties of reading, spelling and arithmetic are being addressed in these games, other skills are developed too. Following instructions in a specific order is an attentional memory skill that is frequently seen to be weak in dyslexic individuals. Poor spelling ability and numerical expertise, as well as other difficulties, can be brought about by weaknesses in sequential memory processing. Playing games practises memory manipulation in a rewarding manner, with information being overlearned repeatedly, stored more reliably in long-term memory, and made it accurately accessible for later use.

Playing in 'a clockwise direction' and integrating with 'the player on your left' helps to reinforce these spatial references. Repeatedly referring to these terms establishes them in the memory, making their meanings more quickly and accurately available at other times.

On a more general note, 'fairness' is a rule of play put into practice to varying degrees. Play which involves interacting with other people allows rules of society to be passed on. Cheating is not allowed, being a bad loser soon loses you friends. The dyslexic child can quickly learn to cheat. It is called 'self-preservation under times of stress'. They may be hiding their reading failure as best as they can – leaving them vulnerable to cries of 'It's not fair' from other players. Cheating must be kept in check, obviously, but if you find your child hooked on deception, it suggests the game is too hard or the child's confidence is weak. As their confidence grows they will not need to cheat, and perhaps begin to learn that preparation and perfected tactics can often pre-empt failure.

Other games provide physical exercise. Inaccurate coordination of eye-hand-foot movements and poor development of fine-motor muscular control hamper the advancement of many skills. Hopscotch, skipping, football, bottle-skittles, jumping, and impersonating a spider (charades?) all provide lessons in physical coordination and control.

Within the home, games of cards, dice and memory can easily be played. Read on to find some examples of these games to play, adapting them as necessary to suit the needs of your individual child.

Card games

Rummy is good for discriminating between numbers, colours and shapes and practises sequencing skills. There are 'rules of play' to be followed and the final scoring of hands where every royalty card is worth 10 points, aces are 15 and every other card is worth five points. Adding up the final scores practises the manipulation of the five times table.

Knock can be played with any number of players. After dealing seven cards to each player, the top card of the remaining pack is then turned over and play begins. The player to the left of the dealer always starts (practises left/right familiarization), and continues in a clockwise direction (as most games do). The object of the game is to have no cards left. In their turn, each player has to play a card that matches either the suit or the number of the previous card. So if the exposed card is the four of hearts, that can be followed by any four or any heart. A player is allowed to play one card. If the player cannot go they must pick up a card off the top of the centre pack. If they can now play, they do so.

When a player has only one card left in their hand, they must 'knock' on the table. If they forget to knock before the next player has their turn, they must pick up three cards as a penalty. Once this level of play has been mastered, extra fun can be introduced by allotting characteristics to different cards; for example:

- Any Jack played changes the suit to the player's choice.

- Any Ace changes the direction of play.
- Play a seven and the next player must pick up an extra card before their go begins.
- Play a two and the next player must also play a two . . . or pick up *two* cards.
- Play a second two. Next player must also play a two . . . or pick up *four* cards, etc.
- An eight played means the next player must miss their go.

This game is excellent for memory practise as well as manipulation of cards. There are tactics of play to be discovered as children become familiar with the game, and as confidence grows, the game becomes a social tool as well as an enjoyable pastime.

Snap is a game we are all familiar with. It can be played with any type of cards (make your own up with words on). *Snap* stirs the brain into making quick decisions based on whole-pattern, shape and colour. When playing with conventional cards, the brain is tuned into the distinctive features of each card, holding that information in short-term memory. If a matching card appears, linguistic skills are called upon in order to yell out 'Snap', again as a result of a rapid mental decision.

All these processes mimic reading tasks: memory, matching and response, based upon inputs received through the visual channel. For a change, try playing the game with spoken words instead, using one player to speak while the others listen for and respond to matching words. The words do not have to be difficult, but they should sound similar if you want your players to work hard for their fun.

Dice games

Angel cakes uses two dice, ten buttons, sweets or other tokens, and two or more players. Each player throws the two dice. Whoever gets the highest score in that round of play 'wins' a token and then throws first in the next round. This game is excellent for familiarizing children with number size and number bonds (for example, $6 + 6 = 12$; $4 + 3 = 7$). Each player counts up their own score – without any hassle from other players! An extra 'twist' can be added by awarding an extra token for anyone who scores 10 with their two dice. (The number bonds that make up 10 are very useful ones to learn.)

Numbers is a brilliant game for two or more players, five dice, and pen and paper. It practises early tables and addition along with all the other facets of communal play. First prepare a score sheet with each player's name and columns for each of the faces of a dice: 1, 2, 3, 4, 5 and 6.

The first player throws the five dice. They then have to decide which ones to keep and which ones to pick up and throw again. After each throw, the player again decides which dice to keep. *After three throws*, the player must decide which squares on the score sheet to fill in (usually determined by which number they have managed to collect the most of).

1st throw of five dice	2	5	5	1	3
keep				5	5
2nd throw of three dice	1	5	6 +	5	5 retained
keep			5 +	5	5
3rd throw of two dice	3	2 +	5	5	5 retained

Score: 5 + 5 + 5 = 15, entered in the '5' column of the score sheet, against player's name

Once a square on the score sheet has been filled in, it cannot be changed. In other words, if I have entered '15' as a result of throwing three fives, I cannot change that to '20' if I should happen to throw four fives later in the game. When the score sheet has been completed, the player with the highest total score is the winner.

There is a game called *Yams* or *Yahtzee* that extends this game, but familiarize yourselves with *Numbers* before tackling more complicated play.

Many board games use dice. Use more than one if possible so that number bonds become familiar. Some shops sell dice with more than six sides enabling more number bonds to be used. You can paint dice yourself to vary their numbers (or add letters or words for other games). For dice games in the car, put cling film over the top of a small plastic pot containing the dice to prevent them jumping out when the pot is shaken. Read the *top* surface of the dice when scoring. This also keeps the dice away from inquisitive toddlers.

Effective strategies for manipulating numbers can be practised with dice. Suppose five dice have been thrown and you need to discover their total score: can the child offer suggestions to make the task easier? One suggestion is to pair up number bonds of 10 (for example, 5+5, 1+9). Another is to line up the dice and count up the dots in groups of three (or any other arrangement), or to sort the dice into groups that share the same number. Problem-solving skills are exercised, approaching a task in different ways and reaching a solution in an achievable manner.

Chance and probability can also be investigated with dice. How many sixes would you expect to have thrown after 12 throws? Is your estimate correct? Perhaps the dice are 'weighted', introducing more words and concepts into the child's growing vocabulary.

Dice can be used to add an element of play to spelling practice. Here is one game suggestion (find another in Chapter 4, 'Spelling issues'). Players spell words of different lengths, according to the roll of the dice. Write game words on cards, labelled on the reverse with the number of letters or syllables contained within them. Use different piles for different players with different spelling abilities and needs. Add foreign words for some players, enabling each player to be challenged and rewarded with the task of play.

Dice games are varied and versatile. With luck, they turn repetitive learning into simple, enjoyable, productive fun.

Memory games

Place six assorted items on a tray. Place the tray in view for twenty seconds. Remove it and ask the players to write down the initial letter of each object *in the right position* on a tray-shaped piece of paper. If that proves easy (for some players), ask them for the first two/three/ four letters, or to spell each word in full. Repeat the game frequently with different types of objects, only increasing the number of objects when six can be remembered with ease.

To improve performance in this game, a player can speak the name of each object (adding a sound/audio element into the sequence being stored for later recall). Alternatively, visual elements of the display can be brought to the mind's attention, providing an extra 'tab' through which the brain can recall the objects displayed; for example, tall (pepper pot), square (sugar cube), spiky (hairbrush), yellow (bottle top), circular (coin).

These tactics may seem obvious, but they are just the type of applicational skills that the dyslexic lacks, which can obviously hamper spelling and reading success. Discover if the player finds one or other of these approaches useful, or confusing. Encourage your players to discover different ways of using their memory, and to apply memory aids to improve their level of success (see also Chapter 11, 'Memory matters').

Talking through the alphabet is a game you may have seen played on TV. The first player speaks a sentence beginning with a word that starts with 'a'. The second player follows on the conversation, introducing their speech with a word beginning with 'b'. This game uses the memory, and considers past and possible forthcoming remarks within the mind.

Memory games involve identifying which specific inputs are useful to store, and which are not. This gives rewarding practice in using, retaining and recalling a variety of material.

When Clare plays *Trix* (see below) with her cousin, she remembers when some cards are played, making remarks such as 'That's the second nine I have played in a row.' If she turns her attention to the aces instead, she will be applying her memory in a way that is more likely to help her win. By noticing when the aces are played. Clare will then be aware which of the Kings in her hand are winning cards.

Trix is a straightforward card game. Players are dealt seven cards, then tricks are won by the highest value card played in each round, the winner being the one to win the most number of tricks. Trumps can be included as players gain proficiency, providing background experience for many other games.

My aunty went to Paris and bought . . . and other similar games utilize memory by requiring the players to recall the ever-increasing list items. Unusual or funny gifts will probably be easier to remember. A distinctive feature noted will prompt memory recall. By helping your child develop memory aids, they have then got experience to use in other situations.

Buzz, pip is a counting game that utilizes memory. To start the game, a player begins with 'one', the next player says 'two', and so on around the team of players. Once the order of play has been established, every number that is a member of the five times table is replaced by the word 'buzz'. Then 'pip' is used as a substitute for every number sharing another small prime factor, such as three. In this case the sequence of play would go: 1, 2, pip, 4, buzz, pip, 7, 8, pip, buzz, 11, pip, 13, 14, buzz-pip, 16, etc. This game is not easy! I would recommend you only use 'buzz' to begin with.

Perhaps, for a change, use body signals: stand up when you speak a number that comes in the three times table. Games like these also show that 'boring' information can have some useful purpose in life, if only to provide family and friends with some entertaining fun!

7

Schooling concerns

Is your school failing your child?

As dyslexic difficulties become apparent, questions need to be asked about the ways in which a school can give their dyslexic pupils access to the curriculum.

Whereabouts in the classroom should a dyslexic child sit? What provision is made to give access to written resources? Is extra time allowed in tests that contain elements of reading and writing? Are there adequate reading books to meet the needs of the dyslexic child? What training and experience have teachers got? Who will explain to the parents what progress a child is making, and which areas require extra input? When will an educational psychologist's report be made? When should a child have a statement of educational needs? How can parents help at home? How much support should be given with homework?

This chapter suggests answers to some of these questions, and outlines the supportive network of specialist help that should be available to the dyslexic child in school. It also introduces the educational psychologist's report which is, at present, almost the only way of clearly identifying specific learning needs.

It is not surprising to find that many dyslexic children hate school. Their vulnerability to confusion, frustration and ridicule requires teachers to be fully aware of any pupil's specific difficulties (and this includes supply teachers brought in to take over lessons). One secondary school I know 'colour codes' the register, ensuring that all staff are constantly reminded of the different needs within each class. In addition, the staff attend regular training sessions to help them 'differentiate' teaching input effectively, and the school has a special needs coordinator who is both experienced and trained.

'Differentiation' is a popular word within teaching circles. It refers to the differing ways teaching material can be adapted or presented to everyone in the class. Different worksheets may be needed for some children. A piece of written instruction may be read aloud by some pupils, for the added benefit of others. So, if your child complains about not understanding, or being left behind in lessons, do not hesitate to talk to the teacher. Perhaps you can both suggest ideas for overcoming an obstacle area in which your child is repeatedly struggling to understand or achieve.

Keep in regular contact with the school, but give them space to apply their training and experience. If you do meet a 'dyslexia-doesn't-exist' type, you can always approach the special educational needs coordinator (or 'Senco', pronounced 'sen-co', if you want to sound informed).

It is sometimes intimidating to approach the school and ask for a quiet word about your child's progress. But if you are concerned, you should make the appointment. And if the school approaches you, don't go in dreading the worst. Teachers are professionals and are used to both children and parents.

Relationships within school

Within the school there are many personal relationships. The relationships a pupil has with teachers are vital, so the teachers must be kept aware of achievement levels in order that comment or correction can be made accordingly. Your child may need homework instructions to be written down to aid their memory; they may warrant preferential access to the teacher when undertaking written work; they may need moving away from the window to reduce distraction. If the teacher is aware of these needs, the child will experience fewer difficulties in class, encouraging a better relationship to develop between the two – a relationship built upon partnership rather than confrontation.

Homework is set by teachers to complement activities undertaken in the classroom. Again, it will help the relationship between pupil and teacher if homework is undertaken and completed on time. If your child is completely unable to achieve something, explain that clearly to the school; but ideally, extract at least part of the task and adapt it to suit your child's ability. For example, if ten pages are required to be read by your child, but they are struggling, offer to read alternate pages. The child will gain from the content of the story, and be encouraged by your support. Make a note on the reading card explaining your actions; then the teacher is aware of the level of progress being made.

If your child works hard on a historical investigation and requires you to be their scribe, let the teacher know. The teacher will be delighted to offer praise for the pupil's contribution and thank you for the necessary homework support you are giving your child.

It is important to point out your child's areas of achievement. They so often face frustration and failure, that they need reminding of the times they can succeed.

Your child will also have many different relationships with other pupils in the school. *Sometimes*, an understanding of dyslexia can help peers understand the trials and tribulations often faced by your child, but more often, a school will encourage a caring, sharing environment in which differences are accepted, and the merits of the individual valued.

Despite this, dyslexic children are often teased at school because of their literacy difficulties. Children can be very cruel to each other and perhaps the only consolation is that those that tease usually have something to hide themselves. A few practised phrases of retort can be useful armoury (the less hurtful the better), and again, remember teachers are used to handling these things and can give you advice.

Child A (non-dyslexic with paint on shirt looking over shoulder of fellow pupil): 'You can't spell "mouse" yet, dork brain!'
Child B (dyslexic): 'Well, at least I know how to wash up a paint pot!'

Supporting school work at home

By keeping in contact with the school, you are best prepared to support your child's learning at home. Perhaps it is a relevant TV programme, library book or conversation. If you know what they are doing at school, you can complement lessons and mimic the 'little and often' method of learning which is shown to be very effective with dyslexic children.

Some dyslexic children can 'access the school curriculum' with just a little extra input from parents, teachers and classroom support. Others need greater resources. It all depends on the degree of difficulty and the personality of the child. Because of the subtle nature of each child's specific learning difficulty, communication with teaching staff who are experienced in these matters is vital for whatever level of support is required.

Whatever provision is made by the school, your child will gain from a sensitive, secure and supportive home. By working together, successes can be achieved. Do not let the homework build up, or confusions fester. Add what you can by keeping records of your child's personal progress, helping everyone uncover and support your child's individual specific needs.

What support should the school be giving?

To help schools monitor and implement support for dyslexic and other children, a Code of Practice exists. This document recommends that parents are kept well informed of events occurring in school, but in reality, most parents find themselves bereft of information. Establish regular contact with the school – perhaps asking to meet the class teacher every term – and then together you can support and understand the progress of your child.

The Code of Practice

The Code of Practice issued under the 1993 Education Act guides schools and local education authorities through the processes involved with the identification and support of pupils with 'special educational needs'. Each school has a policy outlining their approach to special educational needs, and a teacher who coordinates the identification, teaching and monitoring of these children. If you are looking at new schools, ask to see both their policy and their special educational needs coordinator.

When a child is first identified as having difficulties in learning, the Code of Practice requires the school to begin investigative and remedial action within the classroom (supported by home activities if required). The pupil is put on to 'stage one' of the procedure and will remain at this stage for a set period of time before an assessment of progress is made. If the input provided has brought the pupil's level of achievement back on schedule, the child can be taken off the 'stages' procedure, or further goals can be set and monitored. If, however, the additional input provided in the classroom (and home) has not had the required effect, the pupil can be moved on to 'stage two'.

'Stage two' involves the expertise of the school's special needs coordinator. An 'individual educational plan' will be drawn up with goals to be achieved in a set period of time, along with details of how these goals are to be accomplished. A review date will be set to see how much progress is being made. Parents will be encouraged to liaise closely with the school in order that both parties are aware of the child's programme of activities.

Reviews of the child's progress should happen frequently; at least once a term. In time, the pupil may be moved back to 'stage one', or on to 'stage three', depending on their progress and/or degree of difficulty.

At 'stage three' (and for some 'stage two' pupils), specialist teaching is made available either at school or at an off-site location where there is the expertise and equipment available to support the child. What type of support they receive will be determined by an educational psychologist (an expert at identifying specific learning difficulties) who will investigate the child's performance levels and learning approach. A report will be made on the child, highlighting strengths and weaknesses in the child's learning profile, and recommending specific remedial input to support the particular learning difficulties identified through the assessment. Once investigations are completed and recommendations considered, it is up to the school, the education authority and yourselves to activate support for your child in light of the report.

By this stage, your child will be becoming more aware of their difficulties and *may* react badly to extra tuition. However, more often, dyslexic children are so overwhelmingly relieved to find that their difficulties stem from the uniqueness of their brains rather than stupidity that they welcome this expert intrusion into their lives. They will also find that through these 'special' lessons, they can achieve success. The challenge of rebuilding or strengthening their self-esteem can then begin.

If 'stage three' intervention does not meet the needs of your child, 'stage four' is entered into. This prepares the way for a 'statement of educational needs' to be drawn up. This 'statement' (what an awful term!), will provide information about the child's needs in school in order that they can have full access to the curriculum. Any provisions required (such as special equipment, extra staff) will be funded by the local educational authority rather than by calling upon the school's personal budget. Every year the 'statement' will be reviewed, and either updated or revoked depending on circumstance. In secondary schooling, a 'statement' allows certain concessions such as extra time in examinations. The more you are involved with the process, the more you will discover what is relevant to your individual child.

A child with a 'statement of educational needs' is at 'stage five' of the staging procedure. The Code of Practice is there to help schools provide suitable support to any child who, for whatever reason, needs special help to make the most of the school curriculum. Unfortunately, the Code of Practice is, at times, an imprecise document and there is a shortage of funding to implement many of its policy directives. However, it is a step in the right direction.

Confusing terminology

The 'stages' mentioned in the Code of Practice should not to be confused with the 'Key Stages' of the National Curriculum, which have a completely different meaning. The Key Stages refer to the educational levels of different teaching material which is presented to children as they pass through school. *All* pupils begin school at Key Stage 1, receiving input that matches their academic needs and abilities. By the time they are 11 years old, pupils will begin Key Stage 3, following material which 11- to 14-year-olds are required to cover.

Modern teaching material is now labelled 'Key Stage 1/2/3, etc.' to indicate the level of its educational content; the label has nothing to do with its suitability, or not, for a pupil at any stage of the Code of Practice.

Additional teaching support from outside school

Sometimes, parents wish to complement the school's provision of support (or compensate for the lack of it) through employing a specialist from outside the school. These specialists fall, roughly, into two categories:

- Those that implement a structured 'academic' input.
- Those that implement a (mostly physical) programme of remediation in order to develop or adapt neurological pathways within the body (for example, occupational and perceptual therapists).

Specialist teachers can obtain their qualifications through a number of ways, their background perhaps being particularly relevant to your child. For example, a speech therapist may gain extra qualifications in order to support specific learning difficulties. Their background expertise will obviously benefit any child who has spoken language difficulties. An educational psychologist's report will recommend what type of specific remediation and support your child requires.

'Academic' tuition follows structured programmes of teaching that gradually build up areas of previous weakness in the performance levels of the child. Such skills as the use of phonics and whole-word approaches to reading, left-to-right tracking, organization, memory and penmanship will be addressed, and homework activities provided to reinforce lesson material. Head teachers will often let private teachers of this type come into school (just as a music teacher often does). This facilitates liaison with mainstream teachers, and allows the child to be taught at a time when they are receptive, avoiding after-school lessons when the child is often tired.

Other remediation comes in many forms, ranging from homeopathy to reflexology, cranial osteopathy, 'brain gym' and nutritional supplements. Each have their own persuasive reports of success and there is no doubt that for *some* dyslexics, these programmes are well worth the money that they usually cost. By discussing these issues with other parents, you can get a better idea of which different intervention techniques might be suitable for your child, and what is available. 'Academic' input will also be needed to support literacy development, but care must be taken not to overload the child with too many overly demanding programmes.

Dyslexia is still under investigation. The fact that every dyslexic individual varies to a larger or lesser extent from their neighbour makes appraisal of different support programmes very difficult. The media is full of ideas, suggestions and panaceas, which are interesting to follow but often ask as many questions as they answer. Sometimes a report will omit certain details about the background to the study, such as not pointing out that the study quoted took place in New Zealand where the educational system and teaching approach are different from those in Britain. At other times a 'breakthrough' is announced without mentioning the fact that actually only one of the four dyslexic guinea pigs triumphed – albeit that their achievements were remarkable.

What parents need to discover is what type of specific learning difficulty *their* child has, and what type of provision will meet their needs. The best way to uncover this information is through an assessment made by an educational psychologist.

The educational psychologist's report

An educational psychologist's report delivers a wealth of information. It ascertains the intelligence quotient (IQ) of the child, and measures their reading and spelling attainment (to see if IQ matches achievement levels). It also uncovers the performance details of underlying processes occurring within the brain; specifically those involved with the acquisition of literacy.

Sometimes schools will arrange for a psychologist to assess your child using whichever professional is associated with their school. Alternatively, parents can arrange for their child to be assessed by a private psychologist. Schools and local support groups can provide you with names of private professionals, but they are always, understandably, wary about recommending one psychologist above another. They do differ, both in price and in how they write their recommendations. The latter may affect the way a school views the report. You have been warned! I suggest that parents talk to the school and to other parents before choosing which educational psychologist to visit, if they do decide to see one privately. It is also quite acceptable to telephone educational psychologists and ask about their prices, lengths of assessments. At £200 plus for a report, it is worth getting one that the school and you yourself are confident in.

If the school and/or you decide your child is to be assessed by an educational psychologist, preparations will be made to collect background information from a number of sources. Details on the child's physical, emotional and academic development will be required along with information concerning the health, eyesight and hearing of the child, plus any other factor relevant to them.

After assessment testing has taken place, the performance results can be used to clarify the learning profile of the child, highlighting areas of strength and weakness. The report also gives benchmark achievement levels. Such information will help everyone see 'behind the scenes', guiding them towards positive understanding, remediation and measured success.

If a child is not achieving literacy skills, it is vital to find out *why*, in order that appropriate teaching input can be provided. The type of support will vary between individuals, which is why it is important that the recommendations on your child's report are accepted by the school, by yourself, and by any other professionals involved with your child.

Obtaining an IQ for an individual is necessary in order to ascertain their 'potential'. If a child has average or above average IQ, we would expect them to master reading, spelling and numerical acumen with relative ease. If their IQ is below average, they can still achieve these skills, but may require additional support in order to do so.

In order to measure IQ, the psychologist uses tests that do not require reading and/or spelling ability. A variety of tests are given to each child to measure the operational ability of different cognitive pathways within the brain. These tests have been extensively 'calibrated' through the comparison of results obtained from a wide range of individuals. In this way, a raw score of '6 out of 20 correct' in a particular test can be converted into a scaled score of '4' by using a table that accounts for the child's age. This scaled score is then known to be representative of an IQ of, perhaps, '81'. If, in another test, the same child's result represents an IQ index of '119', the psychologist is then aware that the specific cognitive skills required to master the first test are (for whatever reason) functioning below the ability of specific skills utilized in the second test. In other words, an area of weakness has been identified.

Some test results, instead of being represented in IQ terms, are scored according to the 'test age equivalent'. The test given to Christopher to assess his verbal reasoning skills gives him a scaled score of '12', equivalent to the ability of 'nine years, six months'. As Christopher is not yet nine years old, we can see that the cognitive pathways involved in verbal reasoning are developing well and functioning efficiently. However, a test on his visual sequencing skills reveals a scaled score of '4', equivalent to the ability of 'six years'. Once again, comparing this result to Christopher's chronological (actual) age of eight years ten months, we can clearly see that the specific cognitive skills involved with visual sequencing are not functioning at the same level as those involved with verbal reasoning.

Christopher's verbal reasoning skills (ability to use sound common sense and explanation of reason) are superior to his visual sequencing skills (ability to retain items of information within the visual memory and repeat them in order). The psychologist is homing in on the precise nature of Christopher's specific learning difficulty.

Important components of the psychologist's report

The psychologist's tests are divided into three types: verbal (spoken) tasks, non-verbal tasks (which use the eyes, but don't involve reading), and literacy and numeracy tasks. The report will state which particular tests have been used, and the results obtained. Sometimes, the report will attempt to explain the testing procedures and terminology, but remember, an educational psychologist's report is written by a professional conversant with a language most of us have never used, let alone understood! Some reports are clearer than others, but first of all you want to look at the summary, any tables of results (where figures can be compared, not necessarily understood), and the list of recommendations. If any of these three factors are missing, get back to the psychologist straight away, and request them.

In the summary, the report will state if there are any discrepancies between the results of different tests used to uncover intellectual abilities. It is these *differences* which highlight your child's areas of weakness or strength. If dyslexic difficulties are identified, an appropriate teaching approach can be put into action. As we have already discovered, no two dyslexic profiles are the same; every combination of ability versus weaknesses is possible. But with a good educational psychologist's report, the details of individual learning profiles can be identified more easily.

Quite often, more than one specific area of weakness is identified, and sometimes the results of some tests will guide the psychologist to recommend additional assessment by another professional. There is often the suggestion that the child is reassessed in twelve months' time, which is particularly relevant if the child is young. Whatever the age of your report it will contain useful information, so keep it safe. Donate a photocopy of all reports to your child's school and try to ensure that all teachers involved with your child's education have looked at and noted the details and the recommendations that have been made.

With a psychologist's report, 'specific learning difficulties' can be identified. Weaknesses within your child's learning profile can be addressed, their strengths utilized, and their confidence reassured that the secrets of their brains have been released, and action is on its way.

Why do psychologists use the term 'specific learning difficulty'?

Having seen how an assessment by a psychologist reveals the learning strengths and weaknesses of an individual, the term 'specific learning difficulty' can be more clearly understood. Christopher has a 'specific' difficulty in learning: a weakness within the cognitive processes involved with visual sequencing makes it difficult for him to manipulate sequential material. In his case, the sequencing of 'thousands, hundreds, tens, units, decimals' has been particularly difficult for him to learn. Clare also has a 'specific learning difficulty', but hers is within the cognitive processes involved with visual discrimination. Clare finds it hard to differentiate between 'house' and 'horse'. She also has a weakness within her short-term visual memory, explaining the type of difficulties she has had learning to read.

As you can see, 'specific learning difficulties' is an appropriate description of both Christopher and Clare's dyslexic difficulties. In addition, when talking to others, the scope of this terminology allows explanations that detail exactly what these children's particular needs will be. The term 'dyslexia' – on the other hand – is less precise, but there is another reason why professionals do not like to hear it used.

'Dyslexia' has generally become a term to explain any difficulty an individual has with reading, spelling, mathematics or memory. However, difficulties like these can have a number of causes such as low IQ, poor teaching input, illness, or a physiological disability; whereas 'dyslexia', as you and I know it, stems from the neurological patterning of the brain.

However, despite accepting the arguments, I remain attached to the use of the term 'dyslexia', if only because the population as a whole understands, roughly, what I mean by it. 'Specific learning difficulty' is a term less widely understood and can be confused with other terms such as 'moderate learning difficulty' (low IQ), or misunderstood to mean other disabilities that have nothing whatsoever to do with dyslexia.

It is often necessary to inform adults in the wider world of your child's specific learning difficulties. Explaining the child has 'a weakness within their audio modality', is more likely to confuse the situation, not clarify it; whereas saying that your child is 'dyslexic, has a problem following more than one or two instructions, can read reasonably well but finds spelling difficult', will define their difficulties with more precision.

It is also often necessary to explain to your child the reason for their difficulties. Then terminology has to be chosen that your child can understand. It is often difficult finding the words to explain to a child why their friends can write with ease, but they can't, or why they are still required to read the books of a reading scheme while other children are allowed to choose other titles. But if the child is already aware of these differences, they will draw their own conclusions unless you provide them with an explanation.

More often than not, children are relieved to discover their difficulties stem from the uniqueness of their brains, rather than stupidity, laziness, or the nightmare referred to that Tom believed in for months. As dyslexic children get older, they will need to use compensatory tactics to reduce the impact of their difficulties on their lives, and as they face the outside world, they will need to be equipped to cope with a variety of unknown situations that await them.

8

The wider world

Where there's a will there's a way.

As children get older, they become increasingly involved with the outside world. Social expectations, rules and codes have to be learnt by us all, but the dyslexic child meets the additional challenge of coping in a society that is heavily reliant on the written word.

You cannot be with your child 24 hours a day, nor should you want to be. At school, at clubs and alone with their friends, they need to discover how to support themselves and how to 'be' themselves. For them, their literacy difficulties are a minor incumbrance. It is usually we parents who elevate dyslexic difficulties and pass on expectations of failure to our children. At school, there can be difficulties, but in the real world, there is ample opportunity to succeed, partake, and develop individual confidence.

By considering the nature of your child, and utilizing social activities to increase their confidence and ability to succeed, dyslexia need not be an obstacle that excludes them. As individuals, dyslexic children need to take part in society, if only to learn how to adapt to it to suit their own particular needs.

At Cubs or Brownies, when travelling by bus or while shopping, entering a competition, viewing a poster, visiting the cinema or zoo – everywhere we go there is written language to comprehend. And when your disability to achieve understanding is largely invisible, as it is with dyslexia, other people can easily be unaware of the confusions or embarrassments you potentially face.

Understanding signs and notices

It is very important for children to recognize signs such as 'EMER-GENCY EXIT', 'DANGER', and 'POISON'. It is also useful for them to recognize 'Ladies' Toilet', 'wet paint', 'closed', 'press for ticket', etc. – notices that are all there expecting to be read. So, whenever you get the opportunity, practise noting signs and discussing their meanings and the variety of displays.

But remember, not all dyslexic children will have the same difficulties. Some will be very good at seeing the format of signs, recognizing that emergency exit signs are usually red, lit and written in capitals. They may not be able to read the instructions provided on a machine, but are happy to deduce solutions through experience or the observation of others. Or, they are good at asking for help and can take on board the explanations provided. Other dyslexic children will shun any situation that challenges their ability to succeed. If suddenly faced by one difficulty, they may then panic sufficiently to reduce even further their chances of success. You know your child. If they tend to feel anxious when asked to perform new tasks, reduce the challenge in whatever way you can, and help them through it. As their experience grows, so will their confidence. As their confidence grows, so will their ability to cope with, or adjust to, the outside world that surrounds them.

Hobbies and interests

Today there are many extra-curricular activities available both in and out of school. As achievements are important to us all, an activity or hobby that your child will find success in can build self-confidence in other areas. Drama groups, swimming clubs, choirs can all boast the accomplishments of children. Drawing, stamp collecting, computer skills can all bring success.

Clare's parents were apprehensive when she asked them if she could join a local drama club. They had seen how her lines had been muddled in the school Christmas play, and her poor record with maths tables and poetry did not bode well for a theatrical future. But Clare signed up, went along with her friend and a highlighter pen (to mark important details in her script), and within a few weeks was reporting her involvement in an Easter production. Clare's parents did mention Clare's reading and memory difficulties to the drama coach, who then made sure Clare was not getting lost during script discussions. But there were no difficulties: Clare utilized all her abilities to overcome her parents' concerns. Yes, perhaps Clare's lines did vary slightly from one performance to another, and once her friend had to push her onto the stage when she missed a cue; but overall, the *meaning* of her lines was correct, her performance was excellent, and the enjoyment achieved by both audience and cast alike made Clare rejoice the day she had joined the drama club.

Sometimes an interest can be encouraged, specifically aimed at improving weak areas of performance. Visits to the swimming baths will help Mark strengthen coordination skills (as will clambering around playground equipment); and an older child like Christopher may find tennis useful too. There is no point in loading the child with over-demanding, unachievable tasks; but if they gain enjoyment and success, encourage their talents.

Membership of a local library encourages a wide variety of books to be discovered. Some librarians run badge-awarding reading clubs, and competitions that carry enticing prizes. If you familiarize yourself with lending material, the library can offer access to information you may need to support the school curriculum, and expose you to unusual publications that may help to capture your child's interest in books.

Supportive aids

Taking a highlighter pen to drama club was a smart move by Clare. A notepad and pencil are also useful things to carry – to write down instructions or to make private notes to yourself about something for later reference. Another useful accessory is a card with name, address and telephone details, which will give a child such as Tom the confidence to approach situations that might ask for such details. When a librarian kindly suggests that Tom fill in his own registration card, or when Christopher is asked to label his luggage for the return trip from Cub camp, the knowledge that they can consult their card if they wish can be enough to reduce panic and allow them to complete the task successfully. They may need to use the card every time, or just under certain conditions. They may want their birthdate on there too, or a pet's name that they find difficult to spell. Each child is different, with different experiences. Encourage them to recognize their specific difficulties, then through preparation or adjustment, problems can be solved or at least reduced.

(To help a child remember a post code, assign words to the letters. For example, BH3 4RS could become Big Hairy 3, 4 Red Smarties.)

Producing our name and address often precedes other reading and writing requirements as we get older. Becoming confident at filling in these details can allow time for the individual to prepare for forthcoming demands. Samantha, at 13 years old, is starting to enjoy filling in forms now that she has practised a few. When faced with a 'real life situation' she will be better prepared to cope.

For the older dyslexic, a card clearly stating that they are dyslexic and may need help with written and reading tasks is useful for visits to the bank or dentist's surgery, where forms may need to be completed. (Cards are available from the British Dyslexia Association, or make your own.) Even if the card is never used, its presence can give the individual confidence to face situations they might otherwise avoid.

Informing others

Brown Owl, the football coach, the music teacher and, perhaps, the local shopkeeper, will benefit from knowing of your child's dyslexia. It will probably have no bearing for the majority of the time, but when the Brownies are asked to recite their eight times table, the footballers given a long list of instructions to follow, the budding musician asked to recall a sequential list of notes, and the shopkeeper confused by the oddities of money presented, the *invisible* nature of dyslexia will not allow these adults to understand why the child is failing when the presented tasks were deemed achievable. To quote a familiar maxim: 'No one would expect a child with a wooden leg to excel at the high jump.' Nor would their parents send them to Brownies without ensuring those in charge were aware of possible limitations.

But the child does not need to be labelled or made to feel inadequate. A quiet word at an appropriate time (out of earshot of any young earwiggers) is all that is needed, with additional reminders if and when you find it necessary.

Your child *will* meet embarrassing, awkward or challenging situations that they have to cope with. It is impossible and undesirable to protect them completely from these, as they will learn valuable lessons from them. But by listening to your child and by looking out for possible pitfalls, together you will be able to reduce the impact of dyslexia on their self-esteem and willingness to participate in different activities.

9

Memory matters

In order to overcome dyslexic difficulties, we must understand the mind.

Having considered how dyslexia affects individuals and their everyday lives, it is time to delve more deeply into the neurological processes behind dyslexia.

It is now known that the root of almost all dyslexias lies within the genes. Similar to the genetic disposition towards musical ability, freckles or height, dyslexia is seen to be the result of physiological development influenced by information stored within the chromosomes. In the case of dyslexia, physiological features within the tissues of the brain are believed to affect the neurologial circuitry governing the acquisition of literacy. These (mostly subconscious) mental processes greatly depend on the efficiency of the memory to absorb, store, manipulate and retrieve specific symbolic material involved with written speech.

This chapter considers ways in which different weaknesses within the memory can be identified. Weaknesses can then be boosted by delivering a structured programme of learning to improve the brain's ability to manipulate material it previously ignored or handled inefficiently. In addition, ineffective neurological pathways can be bypassed by utilizing an individual's learning strengths.

Introducing the memory

The memory is a complex interaction of neurological processes. We are far from understanding how it really works, but we are closer to identifying how specific weaknesses hamper the abilities of dyslexic children. By using a model of memory – simplifying the details of its complex system – I hope to give you an outline of some possible processing weaknesses occurring within the brain that many believe explain the specific learning difficulties of dyslexic children.

If we consider the memory as a collection of smaller memories, each connected to each other through neurological pathways and other processing units of the brain, we can begin to understand how an 'unusual' wiring of these pathways could lead to a distinct variation in the processing style of the brain. There are also short-term and long-term elements in this collection or 'body' of memories. A Short-term (or working) memory is where inputs are considered, filtered, rejected or stored. Long-term memory units store selected elements of information. The transference of material between short-term and long-term memory is clearly of significant importance if the code of written language is to be learnt. In order for reading and spelling to occur, memories of previous experience of written and spoken words are required. For the dyslexic child, the processes which either store or recall these vital memories are, for whatever reason, working ineffectively. Their neurological pathways have been wired in an unusual manner.

Reading and spelling are just two of the skills that utilize the memory, selectively storing and retrieving information relevant to the task in hand. Sequencing, predicting and mathematical computation also rely on the accuracy and speed of memory processing. So, when considering the types of specific difficulties faced by dyslexic individuals, weaknesses within the storage and retrieval mechanisms of the memory are usually found.

Identifying specific weaknesses

There are four areas of memory most commonly associated with dyslexia: the audio memory, the visual memory, the semantic memory (where word meanings are stored) and the working memory (where active thought occurs).

Weaknesses within a processing channel can be identified by a lack of data available to support relevant tasks. For example, if 'sniff' is spelled 'snif', we can suspect that the *visual* memory has not registered the double 'f'. By collecting together errors produced by a child, along with their achievements, we can begin to identify areas of weakness and strength within their learning profile.

Despite the fact that a weakness in one processing channel will put extra demands upon other neurological processes, blurring precise details, the following profiles should nevertheless help you achieve an indication of your child's specific difficulties that require your specific support.

In Chapter 1, we looked at the characteristics of six dyslexic profiles. This chapter considers their cases again, but looks at the causes behind their difficulties, relating findings more specifically to the processes occurring within the mind.

I should point out that not everyone will agree with this isolation of disabilities, preferring to treat dyslexia as a 'whole' disorder. But I have found that by attempting to identify weaknesses, learning *strengths* can also be revealed; and that parents, teachers and the child can grasp a better understanding of the tasks required in order to overcome specific difficulties by classifying the learning process.

Weaknesses within the audio memory

A weakness within Samantha's audio memory (where sounds are stored) is revealed when she spells. She writes 'could' with ease, but struggles to produce the word 'stoon' (an invented word). 'Could' has an 'odd' spelling (it is an odd bod as defined in Chapter 4), i.e. the sound of the word does not match its letters, so it can only be spelled correctly through memory traces which recall the visual details of the written code. 'Stoon' can be spelled by translating component sounds into a letter-code whose rules, though complicated, can be learnt. This is called phonetic coding. By informing Samantha that 'stoon' is an invented word, she knows that she has to create it using sound-to-letter group knowledge alone. Proficient spellers use both phonological and visual memories to create unfamiliar words. They would have no difficulty in translating the sounds of 'stoon' into its st-oo-n components. If presented with an unfamiliar word to spell, such as 'enticing', they would be able to recognize that both 'inticing' and 'entising' were visually incorrect (depending on their age and reading experience).

Samantha's ability to spell 'could' suggests that her visual memory can provide her with details of a word she has seen before. (One could never *guess* the spelling of 'could'.) However, her audio memory, where sounds of letters and letter-groups are stored, is unable to provide the necessary information to construct a word from sound alone. She produced 'ston' – showing there is access to some sound-to-symbol knowledge, but not in regard to the 'oo' sound.

Weaknesses within the visual memory

Clare has an opposite problem. She can spell 'stoon' with ease, but 'could' has not registered as a word assembled of 'unusual' letters. She produces 'cood', matching the sounds of the word with sound-to-letter group knowledge stored and retrieved from her auditory memory. Her visual memory may lack all ability to provide Clare with the memory trace of 'could'. Another possibility is that it is attempting to, but Clare's auditory memory is 'swamping out' the messages. Either way, the processes behind her visual memory can be considered as 'weak'.

Weaknesses within the semantic memory

Clare also has difficulties with the fluidity of her speech. Her conversation is peppered with 'thingy', 'what-der-yer-call-its' and close but incorrect versions of words she knows, but is unable to recall with ease. This is very tiring for both Clare and her listeners. She seems to have difficulty accessing names accurately from her memory, but can tell you that the 'thingy' is used for finding your way, is black and round, she had it yesterday out in the garden – ah yes, a compass. These difficulties are characteristic of a weakness within the semantic memory where meanings of words, and associated words, are stored.

Inefficient storage and retrieval of names is a common feature of dyslexics. Most of us can appreciate this difficulty because we all experience it sometimes, but when it extends to the naming of a banana, we know that we are witnessing a serious obstacle. Another feature of poor semantic memory is its weak grasp of intangible concepts such as 'bravery' or 'elegance'. The individual may know the use of a word, but when asked to express its meaning, they find it difficult.

In order to keep up the flow of speech, it is believed that the brain is 'prompted' to access words that may be called upon by the speaker. So if 'lamb' is mentioned, associated language such as 'fluffy', 'bleat' or 'mint sauce' may come to mind. Similarly, when reading, a word in the text will 'prompt' the brain into expecting associated words, and so allow the recognition of these words to occur much faster. These associated words are 'waiting in the wings', in preparation for their possible arrival.

The use of the semantic memory when reading allows greater access to the meaning of the text. Not only will the reader be gaining purpose and understanding, but the brain will be 'prompted' into the expectation of forthcoming text. If you understand what you are reading, your mind is primed and positively 'on the look out' for associated words.

71

Weaknesses within the working memory

Mark, who is four, displays behaviour that at times suggests a weakness within his working memory. Given more than one task to do – such as looking at the pictures while listening to the story – he seems unable to execute these things together. He comments on the picture in a manner that suggests he has taken in little, if any, of the explanatory text. Or, if he is asked to collect his coat and scarf, he returns with one, having forgotten the other. But Mark is only four years old. Many children of his age have not developed the ability to perform more than one task at a time. There is time yet for Mark to master these skills, but imagine the effect of this weakness if it did persist into school.

As Christopher manipulates mathematics, his working memory will be full of conscious and subconscious thoughts. If a blackbird starts to shriek outside the window, his working memory will have even more information to contend with.

Most children handle a number of stimuli simultaneously, or manage to screen out unnecessary ones. Many dyslexics, however, when manipulating material known to be specifically difficult for them, are vulnerable to both interference and distraction from other stimuli.

The working memory is like a motorway service station! Many different stimuli pass in and out, processed in many different ways along the way. If the lorry park is too small, or the toilets badly signposted, all manner of immediate and knock-on events will affect the system. Within the working memory, inefficient processing can miss inputs, store them defectively, or confuse them with other material that is being processed at the same time.

If lists of instructions are quickly forgotten, if spoonerisms ('spucket and bade') frequently occur, or the child seems unable to attend to one topic for any length of time, a weakness within the working memory could be suspected.

Attention Deficit Hyperactive Disorder

Weaknesses within the working memory are also identified in children diagnosed as having an Attention Deficit Hyperactive Disorder (ADHD). This hampers their ability to attend to more than one task at a time, and often presents them with a difficulty in differentiating between important and insignificant stimuli.

Clearly, there is an overlap between the profile of some dyslexic children and those with ADHD; but that does not mean that dyslexia and ADHD are one and the same thing. Instead, it calls for careful diagnosis in order that appropriate support can be given. Many children with attentional difficulties still manage to achieve literacy skills and do not display the typical errors produced by the dyslexic. Some dyslexic children can focus their attention without falling prone to distraction (at least to the level one would expect of any child not suffering an attentional difficulty), and have neither the hyperactive nor passive reaction to the surrounding environment that can be witnessed in children with attentional disorders.

I have included the address of an organization involved with ADHD at the end of this book for those who wish to discover more about this particular condition.

What to do next

By carefully considering the nature of your child's performance errors (and/or by reading an educational psychologist's report), individual weaknesses and strengths become apparent. This indicates the type of learning experience that they will require to support success.

For example, Samantha now knows she has a weakness within her audio memory. She understands why lectures that deliver information largely through the spoken word leave her with little understanding of their content, and now knows the importance of work-sheets, of reading-up a subject in a book, and of making pictorial revision sheets which will help her revise by utilizing strengths within her visual memory instead.

So, in order to support your child effectively, you need to identify which areas of *their* memory are susceptible to inefficiency in order that you can supply appropriate inputs and alternative routes to success.

Improving performance weaknesses

Having seen where and how weaknesses can be identified, we can consider methods that will improve the way in which the storage and retrieval of information to and from specific areas of the memory can be *improved*.

There are a number of ways that we can do this. As these are some of the methods by which specialist teachers increase the abilities of dyslexic children, it will be useful for you to read and consider the following suggestions, in order to understand the purpose behind much of the specialist teaching material. If these methods are to work, teaching input needs to be applied repeatedly (that means daily either at home or in school), revised frequently, and actually *used* by the child. Without active participation at home, these conditions are hard to achieve.

Enhancing inputs to improve memory skills

In order to improve the memory of a dyslexic child, it is advisable to present learning experiences in very vivid ways. Thus the child's full range of senses can be involved. The idea is that the experience is so strong that even if the child forgets some aspects of it, the central concept is likely to be retained. Repetition and practice will be needed too.

Supporting the audio memory

Use colour to highlight phonemes (chunks of sound) within words. Present words in groups that share the same sound-to-symbol pattern. Speak a word; request its spelling. Use letter-sounds rather than letter-names. Practise putting letters together to make sounds. Encourage the breaking down of words into smaller, familiar chunks.

Another good exercise for the audio memory is the spelling of invented words. By reducing the ability for the visual modality to reproduce the written word through its shape (because the eyes have never seen the word written before), the writer must call heavily upon the audio modality and its store of sound-to-letter groupings. By practising the process of building up invented words, spelling skills can be learnt and transferred to the spelling of non-invented words that share the same letter-to-sound patterns within them. Reading invented words also homes in on the skill of decoding words into sound chunks. Although you don't want to fill your child's head with too many invented words, do play with letters together, and show them how much expression can be achieved through the combination of sounds.

'Glumpy' could be the name of a monster that looks both grumpy and lumpy. 'Shox' may be the invented name of a story-character. Such harmless fun exercises the transformation of words into a language of letters. This, after all, is a skill dyslexic children find

74

difficult, so they need achievable practice in order to improve their abilities.

Furthermore, as dyslexic children daily face the challenge of writing words they cannot spell, requiring them to invent spellings frequently, they have to have some knowledge of a *feasible* combination of letters that will portray the sounds of the word they wish to express in order that their reader will understand their attempt. Generally speaking, it is easier for a reader to decode an unknown word through sound. Therefore it is better that a child writes 'cuberd' instead of 'cbol' when 'cupboard' is intended – making an attempt to use the audio modality to create a spelling the dyslexic may, or may not, know they are unable to spell.

Supporting the visual memory

Add colour. Bring attention to distinctive visual elements within a word. Highlight words within words. Show a word, remove it, request its spelling. Use artwork to highlight spelling details. Practise reading single words in isolation, away from meaningful text.

To exercise the visual memory specifically, copying tasks can be incorporated into play. When a player throws an even number on a dice, they can copy one line from an eight-lined design that is either on display before them or shown and then removed from sight. Use straightforward designs and encourage the child to tackle the task in an organized fashion.

Playing 'spot the difference' and finding hidden objects within pictures are also good exercises for the visual memory. For revision tasks at school, display material in picture form rather than in words, using colour and humour to stimulate clear memory traces within the visual modality.

Supporting the semantic memory

Present a word; collect associated words. Remove a key word from a sentence, let child guess the missing word. Discuss content of material before reading or writing to support understanding. Recap material frequently, and predict forthcoming events.

Supporting the working memory

Reduce number of tasks presented simultaneously. Organize tasks into achievable units. Define sequence of events. Use memory aids to help transfer material effectively into long-term memory units.

It has been shown that *remembering* a memory strengthens the memory traces better than purely seeing/hearing/experiencing the input again.

A multisensory approach

There are other areas of memory – such as those of smell, touch and colour perception – which can and should be incorporated into the learning process. The memory is a living integration of many parts. For example, it is possible to use the sensation of touch to write words in sand or salt. By also singing out the word as it is created, a multisensory input is produced which will help fix the word in the memory.

Many teachers use multisensory learning techniques, and educational psychologists will often recommend these methods for dyslexic children. The theory is that by bombarding as many senses as possible with the same information, the almighty weight and variety of material presented is sure to be registered somehow, somewhere. The trick is to provide an assortment of activities that use different senses, but not to overload the working memory by giving too much at one time. Spread out your multisensory inputs rather than deliver them all at the same time.

Utilizing strengths

By observing your child's working and learning profile, strengths as well as weaknesses will be uncovered. By positively utilizing and developing strengths, the impact of weaknesses can be reduced, circumventing the processing channels that are seen to bring confusion and error. By both boosting the ability of failing channels and adapting reliable channels to compensate for weaknesses elsewhere, the individual is better equipped to face the variety of demands placed upon them. To improve existing strengths within the various channels of the mind, apply the same sort of 'supportive tactics' as listed above.

Clare, therefore, can be encouraged to utilize her visual memory, particularly by techniques such as word dissection, and by using colour to pick out parts of words with similar sounds, which will improve her ability to learn and recall spelling patterns and word shapes. But she will also be introduced to tactics (such as the mispronunciation of particular words to highlight oddities within their spelling, such as knife), that will relieve the pressure upon her weaker visual channel by utilizing the strengths she has in her audio memory.

In order to establish secure memory traces, inputs will need to be repetitively presented to the dyslexic mind, and constantly recalled over time. Present the same material in different ways and use it in different situations, if necessary using memory aids and tactics to support success.

Tactics and aids

We all use memory aids of different types: a shopping list, an address book, a knot in the handkerchief. A dictionary is a memory aid, providing you are practised at using it efficiently. A table square, an address card, a notebook and pencil to hand – all service the dyslexic's need to support their memory.

Playing a game repetitively helps the memory by reducing the novelty of material to be handled. The dyslexic can then gain in confidence, partake in a social skill, and even receive positive approval and admiration for competing well. Remember, it does not have to be Bridge to be enjoyable, competitive and skilful. Choose games that are within the memory capacity of your child. Even a 'simple' task such as identifying between a 'P' and a '9' can take a long time to root itself in the memory. Repetitive and meaningful input is required, preferably delivered through the eyes, ears, mouth (speech) and touch.

As players become proficient with any type of game, tactics can be developed. Dyslexics are usually exceptionally good at developing tactics, for two reasons. First, they are often positively looking for strategies that will aid their success. (These may be called 'cheating' or 'good use of initiative' depending on circumstance and attitude of the judge!) Second, due to the nature of their dyslexia, they often 'see' things in a way slightly different from other individuals, causing them to approach some tasks in an unusual manner.

Tactics are the means by which obstacles are overcome. To recall the spelling of 'witch', for example, a picture can be used – if the cross stroke on the letter 't' is drawn to show a broomstick (and a witch on the broomstick) then this helps the child associate the spelling with the concept.

Before reading a passage of writing, scanning through the text to identify a few of the long words is a tactic to increase the fluidity of reading, and also to encourage contextual understanding. When writing a story, a plan will organize and consolidate ideas.

Dyslexics need to understand and develop tactics. They also need to understand how *they* learn. By viewing the tasks undertaken by your child; implementing support and reducing obstacles; and encouraging strategic consideration of how success can be best achieved, you are developing a *positive* outlook to dyslexia, and helping your child to do the same.

10

Positive outlook

Successful people need the individual confidence to be themselves.

You may be wondering what positive aspects there can be to dyslexia. This book highlights numerous situations in which the dyslexic child is disadvantaged, where dyslexia hampers their everyday lives and when others around them are confused and dismayed. As a 'hidden' condition, with many variations, dyslexia cannot be measured precisely nor its effects determined with ease. It cannot be 'cured' either, only supported, and its impact reduced. A gloomy outlook for the dyslexic child and their family – or is it?

The child may not see the announcement of dyslexia as a problem. They may be relieved, even delighted to discover their difficulties are not their fault, that their mistakes are not due to stupidity or laziness. They will find parents and teachers become more understanding, hopefully providing support that reduces their experience of failure and rejection, enabling them to achieve success.

'Dyslexia' describes a condition caused by unusual processing abilities within the brain. By harnessing these abilities, the dyslexic can achieve unusual feats, rewarding them with alternative routes to success. But what level of success can be reached by a dyslexic child?

Reading

Most dyslexic children *can* learn to read. Their progress is likely to be slow and irregular, constantly requiring support and encouragement during their early school years. With appropriate teaching, all but the most severely dyslexic can achieve sufficient reading skills to handle the basic reading requirements of secondary school. This does not necessarily mean they will be 'good' readers, or even eager readers; they will need continued support when faced with new words, and are likely to perform badly when under stress, but the process of decoding the written word can (almost always) be achieved.

Every child is different. Samantha's breakthrough to reading came when, instead of breaking words down into sounds, her parents 'gave' her the whole word whenever she came to a reading obstacle. Samantha's visual vocabulary of reading words increased although it did lead to errors between similarly spelled words. After a boost from this approach, Samantha followed a phonics programme which increased her knowledge of letter-groupings (for example '-tion', '-ally', 'oa'). She was taught positive, word-attacking strategies to use when faced with an unknown word. This enabled Samantha to break words down into smaller units, decode them into sound, and build them up. She received support that improved the ability of her weak audio memory, and as a result was able to increase her store of recognizable visual patterns to store in her long-term visual memory.

Clare whispers to herself when she reads alone. The sound of the words helps her to access their meaning through the abilities of her audio memory, supporting weaknesses within her visual modality, and bringing her success.

When reading to themselves, both Samantha and Clare are relieved the task of translating the written word fully into speech. Without this added burden (which is particularly great if their audiences are poised to leap upon mistakes), they are able to access the meaning of text more clearly. This, after all, is the purpose of reading. But both these children needed support in order to increase their reading vocabulary and experience of the written word with all its punctuation and grammatical subtleties. So shared reading exercises are required, but private reading should also be encouraged. As these children get older, they will continue to ask for decoding help, but they will also become more confident and apt at deciphering written language for themselves.

Spelling

Dyslexic children rarely grow up to be excellent spellers. Even words that seem established securely in their long-term memory can suddenly lose their correct sequence of lettering, and spelling errors can reappear despite intensive efforts to remove them. However, with the advent of computer technology, the telephone and support from dictionaries, spelling aids and helpful friends, the dyslexic need not face exclusion because they cannot spell. Many stories circulate of dyslexic business men (and probably women), whose secretaries screen out mistakes that might otherwise expose their spelling weaknesses. These business people are successful, able to adapt either their environment, or themselves, to succeed.

Motivation

Sometimes we witness a dyslexic child struggling with literacy and wonder how we would cope with similar difficulties ourselves. I suspect I would be one of the first to throw the book across the room, or snap my pencil with frustration. Sometimes such behaviour is witnessed, but more often (provided the child is encouraged and presented with achievable targets to reach), the dyslexic pupil will attend to the task in hand, motivated by a desire not to face further failure.

From an early age, dyslexic children may face frustration and failure caused by their specific learning difficulties. We would like to avoid it, but reality tells us that if you live in a largely literate society, and go to school where literacy is both taught and assumed, then at some time or another a lack of literacy will lead to embarrassment, frustration, confusion and failure.

However, if you watch many dyslexics as they grow older, you see their early experiences of disappointment have sometimes left them better prepared to tackle difficulties ahead. The alternative ways in which they learn, and their past experiences, leave them better equipped, or determined, to overcome obstacles of many different kinds. They are used to problem-solving and hard work – often more so than some of their non-dyslexic peers who did not meet such challenges at such an early age.

Self-esteem

Unfortunately, some children react to the demands of society by rejecting it. Sometimes other difficulties alongside dyslexia hamper progress still further. And for some, overt messages from surrounding people so reduce their confidence that insecurity itself becomes another cause of failure.

It is therefore very important to maintain or rebuild the dyslexic child's self-esteem. By developing strengths within themselves, and putting literacy difficulties into perspective (there are a whole lot of things that are worse than not being brilliant at reading, spelling and perhaps arithmetic), the child is encouraged to face their difficulties from a positive angle.

Confidence

As self-esteem grows, so will confidence in their ability to tackle and achieve. Obviously, confidence is a delicate condition, particularly for the dyslexic who has been sensitized by past experience. This can also mean that the dyslexic 'latches on' to situations they feel confident with, finding it hard to venture on to unfamiliar ground, be it attending a new club or attempting a new book. However, with support and experience, they can discover their ability to extend their experiences of life.

As they develop strengths within their character, and improve their abilities in areas far removed from the written word, they can achieve exceedingly high results through determination to satisfy their self-esteem. As a result, they can gain in confidence, fuelling their ability to achieve personal merit.

Clare is exceptionally good at verbal reasoning. Why do we put stamps on letters? How can we get the lamb and the lion across the river with only one boat? She may not always be good at expressing her answer, but she can reason and solve problems very well. This will set her in good stead for her older years, but even now she is beginning to show her talents during class and family discussions.

Jonathan is developing his artistic skills and achieving excellent results, often surprising his audience with his unusual displays that capture his desire to express his ideas. Jonathan's artistic success has increased his interest in art, giving his parents and teachers a 'way in' to many other topics.

At the age of thirteen, Samantha can speed-read faster than her mother. This has been something of a surprise for them both, but only through the maturity of her years has Samantha uncovered her talent, and recognized it for what it is. She reads in a manner different from her mother.

After speed-reading a page, both mother and daughter are asked a number of questions. Mum answers correctly, almost repeating word-for-word the relevant section of the text. Samantha produces slightly different replies. When Mum says, 'The girl is wearing a frilly pink dress', Samantha says, 'The girl is wearing pretty clothes.' Samantha has not decoded or remembered the text word-by-word, but has assimilated its overall meaning. This method of reading may not always be suitable (she may need to slow down, even ask for decoding help, when faced with unknown words), but it gives Samantha access to a wealth of texts she was unable to access before. Samantha has developed an individual style of reading that brings her success.

Individuality

Dyslexic children are individuals. What makes their individuality slightly different from that of their peers is that the dyslexic child is usually aware of their singularity from an earlier age. As they begin their schooling – integrating with their peers, learning their way towards independence – they soon discover that they are, in some way, 'different'. This feeling of difference can stay with them for many years, moulding their attitudes, personality and integration with the outside world.

Fortunately, British society accepts individuality. Providing certain rules are not overstepped, the entrepreneur, the outstanding employee, the unusual character is not ostracized from the 'average, normal, non-distinctive' population. In fact, others, quite often, positively welcome their alternative view upon life.

Along with the musically gifted, the athletic and the classroom swot, the dyslexic child is the product of the brains and brawn they possess and have been able to use through opportunities provided by the world around them. So, rather than observing the dyslexic as an 'incomplete' individual, through their lack of acumen in literacy, they should be recognized as unique individuals possessing an unusual ability to process neurological data in an alternative way to others. They have a hidden potential to observe and perform tasks in an original manner not available to their non-dyslexic peers.

While parents need to appraise and implement programmes of remedial support, they should also consider the merits of their individual child. Wherever possible, they should allow them to develop confidence in themselves, rather than forever being presented with an idealized preference for achievements that they *might* have gained had not dyslexia affected their destiny.

Albert Einstein left school at 14, unable to read, much to the dismay of his father. The parents of Hans Christian Andersen, Eddison, and Leonardo da Vinci (to mention just a few), were probably equally disappointed by their offspring's dyslexic disabilities. Yet they survived, along with the many other dyslexics who did not make it into the history books.

How common is dyslexia?

Through history books, autobiographies and the media, we can find many examples of dyslexic people. Among family and friends, dyslexic tendencies are frequently found, particularly as the details of its identification become clearer, and the topic becomes discussed with open veracity. It sometimes makes me wonder who among us does possess 'the perfect brain'!

Governments have attempted to measure the incidence of dyslexia within the classroom, and other bodies have produced figures from studies of their own. As many as 20 per cent of children appear in these reports, exhibiting varying types and degree of specific learning difficulty. The size of this figure may surprise some people, but its presence suggests: (a) dyslexia is on the increase; and/or (b) we are better at identifying it; and/or (c) the teaching methods presently employed in the classroom do not suit the learning style of the dyslexic pupil, leading to an increased number of 'borderline' pupils falling into the failure zone.

Whatever the facts are, we can be assured that our children are not alone with their dyslexic angle on life. They *can* learn, and so can we – replacing confusion with consideration and positive aspirations.

11

Activities

This chapter outlines various activities designed to help the dyslexic child. At the end of the book are further sources of information. This book is merely the tip of an iceberg . . . Bon voyage!

Dyslexic children often find spelling difficult. They need guidance to help them structure their attempts; rules which bring attention to the symbol-to-sound relationships between letters; and games which put these lessons into practice.

The -ing game

There are two rules associated with the addition of '-ing' to a word:

1 *-ing* eats the 'e' off the end of the root word, for example shake:shaking.
2 The end consonant must be doubled if there is a 'high' vowel sound *immediately* before that last consonant, for example, sit:sitting.
   Players throw the dice and move around the board, adding *-ing* at the end of each go:

- If *-ing* eats an 'e' – go backwards two spaces.
- If *-ing* doubles a consonant – go forwards two spaces.
- If no change occurs when -ing is added – stay still.

Having moved according to these instructions, your go is over. Play moves to the next person. The player who reaches the end first is *the winner* (see Figure 1).

Quizzes of different types

Dyslexic children frequently need to use and revise material a number of times before it becomes established in their long-term memory. By creating your own trivia questions, general knowledge and lessons from school can be overlearned successfully. Children can read questions to others too, after practising them beforehand if necessary, with or without your help.

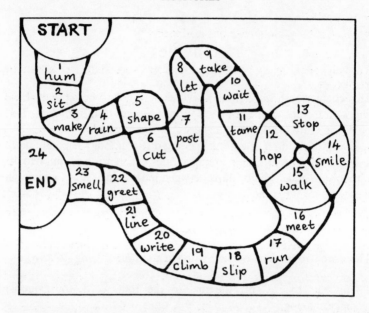

Figure 1   Board for the -ing game

- What is the capital city of France?
- What is a baby cow called?
- Who has the longest name in this room?

For questions whose answers may not be readily known, choices can be given:

- Which planet is nearest the sun? Earth/Jupiter/Mercury.
- How many legs does an octopus have? eight/six/two.
- What relation is Graham to Geoffrey? uncle/niece/nephew.

Another method of incorporating quizzes into play is to devise treasure hunt clues where answers are needed to move the players on.

Write down the first letter of each answer. Make a word to tell you where to find your next clue:

- The opposite of white is? b
- Which fruit did Eve share with Adam? a

- How old is Rita? t
- What is the eighth letter of the alphabet? h

To help spelling and reading, other treasure hunt clues can be fashioned to suit your needs:

Write down the missing letters to find where your next clue hides: 'Sim*le Simon met a p*em*n, goi*g t* the fair' — — — — —

To practise single-word reading (reading words out of context), a trail that leads them from item to item will lure them into learning. Write the word 'telephone' clearly and display it to the players. By the telephone, place a card with 'fruit bowl' written on it. In the fruit bowl, leave a card with 'linen cupboard' on it, and so on. You can help children write clues for each other, giving a purpose to writing and accurate spellings.

They might also enjoy playing charades where the names of books/films/television programmes are considered beforehand and then written on slips of paper to be randomly selected by players. *Any* type of writing practice is valuable: shopping lists, requests for Santa, playful or serious menus, words of a song. Every word need not be spelled correctly. It is the *purpose* and *enjoyment* received that will spur them on to do more.

Telling the time

As mentioned in Chapter 3, many dyslexics find telling the time difficult. Time is expressed by complicated symbols and language. With its display variations and terminology, time presents the dyslexic (and many others) with a number of areas where mistakes and misunderstandings can easily be made.

The digital clock is now a familiar sight, on the video recorder, microwave and radio alarm. It can represent either the 12- or 24-hour day and may display time purely as a numerical fact. The analog clock, however, has a completely different display, adding a spatial dimension to the observance of time, and has different terminology to go with it. Once the child understands the principles behind these displays, they are better equipped to access and utilize the various timing devices around them.

To help your child grasp understanding it is necessary to identify the components of the clock, and discover the purpose of each in isolation, perhaps with a 'tab', so that future consultations of the clock can utilize, and build upon, previous lessons.

Analog time display

The minute hand is the long one – it is a long arm, matching its long name.

The hour hand is the short one – it is a short arm, matching its short name.

Once the child can differentiate between the two hands and has been shown their directional movement, then the task of explaining how these hands indicate time can begin.

The biggest confusion dyslexics usually have to begin with is which hand points to what. The numerals around the edge of the clock face are confusing. The child needs, crucially, to understand that these digits as *numbers* have absolutely nothing to do with the minute hand. To explain this, here are two storylines that act as an introduction to the part played by the hour and minute hands on the clock.

Storyline to explain how the minute *hand is read*

The minute hand rushes around the clock face quite fast. Follow its progress during tea or over the half-hour duration of a television programme to show how fast it moves compared to the hour hand. It is moving so fast that it does not 'read' the numbers around the edge; the long minute hand ignores them as it hurries on its way. When we want to find out how far around the clock face the minute hand has travelled, we count the 'dashes' around the edge.

Storyline to explain how the hour *hand is read*

The short, slow, hour hand does not dash around the clock face. It moves very slowly, taking all morning just to get around the clock face once. As it is going so slowly, it has plenty of time to pay attention to the numbers around the edge, and sometimes even has a bell rigged up to celebrate its arrival at each new number. It takes all morning for the hour hand to travel once around the clock – from twelve o'clock midnight to twelve o'clock midday. It then takes all afternoon for the hour hand to travel around the face again from twelve o'clock midday to twelve o'clock midnight. So, *one whole day*, from midnight through midday and on to the next midnight, involves two 12-hour circuits of the hour hand – 24 hours altogether.

By making three clock faces out of cardboard – one to show the minute hand only (no digits, only dashes), one to show the hour hand only and one to show both hands – the separate movements of the hands can be illustrated first, and then displayed together in the conventional manner. By repeatedly operating these models, the child can practise representing events such as '34 minutes past six o'clock', and then be introduced to variations in terminology (for example, '6:34 or 26 minutes to seven o'clock'.

Now it is possible to look at the digital display and show how he numbers there are representing time.

Digital time display

Terminology required to express the time in a digital number is more straightforward than that used by the analog display. For example, 06:45 is expressed as 'six 45'. (Phrases such as 'quarter to seven' are products of an analog upbringing.)

With many digital clocks displaying 24 hours, '14:34' and similar times need to be understood, along with 'a.m.' and 'p.m.' for those clocks that only register numbers up to 12. The value of 60 seconds and 60 minutes; a quarter, half and three-quarters of an hour; and the judgement of time periods such as 'ten minutes', need to be learnt through frequent time-keeping exercises of different types – once again, using understanding and practice to consolidate learning.

Poster idea

By making a picture that can contain words that share a spelling pattern, the child can enjoy the challenge of filling the poster. For example, the spelling pattern 'oa' can be shown on a poster of a goat in a boat, with many other words that share the 'oa' spelling pattern written on the side of the boat (see Figure 2). Use colour to highlight sound bites within words. By displaying the work, the words can be frequently considered and discussed. After a week, see how many words off the poster the child can remember.

Sliders

Chunking words down into smaller sound bites familiarizes the dyslexic child with common phonemes (units of sound). This knowledge supports the development of both spelling and reading skills.

Figure 2   Goat in a boat poster

Sliders are an enjoyable and versatile resource that encourages the awareness of phonemes. I have outlined their production below, but vary their format to suit your needs.

Fold one piece of card and cut a window out of it.

Staple along one edge and write an 'onset' (initial sound) in clear lettering on the card.

Cut a strip of card. Ensure it 'slides' through the folded card smoothly.

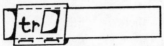

Write down a number of word endings that match your chosen onset, noting that onset on the back for future use.

> *ain   ail   ait*

Show the child both halves of the slider. Practise reading the phonemes in isolation before putting the slider together and reading the whole word.

> *ain* | **tr** *ail* | *ait*

Sliders may also be used with simple maths. The solution to several different sums could be shown to be the same number. Children can make their own sliders providing they check that spellings and facts are correct before committing them onto card.

Common words

Here is a bank of 200 common words that your child should be able to read and spell. Add to it the child's names, address details, names of friends and relations, pets, hobbies and any other key words they repeatedly use.

Make two copies of the completed lists: one for recording spelling achievements on, and one to monitor reading. When a word has been read or spelled correctly, place a dot beside that word. Three dots allows the word to be removed from the list and another one added. Additionally, compile another list that includes key words for school subjects with the help of your child's teacher(s).

These lists enable both children and adults to identify which words are beneficial to learn, and can be used to set spelling achievement goals.

a	if	that	best	let	think
about	in	the	bird	live	three
all	into	their	black	long	time
an	is	them	blue	man	too
and	it	then	boy	many	tree
are	just	there	bring	may	under
as	like	they	day	men	us
at	little	this	dog	mother	very
be	look	to	don't	Mr	walk
back	made	two	eat	never	white
been	make	up	every	next	why
before	me	want	fast	once	wish
big	more	was	father	open	work
but	much	we	fell	own	woman
by	must	well	find	play	would
call	my	went	five	put	yes
came	no	were	fly	ran	year
can	not	who	four	read	
come	new	what	found	red	months
could	now	when	gave	room	days
did	of	where	girl	round	seasons
do	off	which	give	run	
down	old	will	going	sat	personal
first	on	with	good	saw	details
for	one	you	got	say	
from	only	your	green	school	
get	or		hand	should	
go	our	after	help	sing	
had	over	again	home	sit	
has	other	always	house	so on	
have	out	am	how	stop	
he	right	ask	jump	take	
her	said	another	keep	tell	
here	see	any	know	than	
him	she	away	last	these	
his	so	bad	left	thing	
I	some	because			

The octopuses' party

Here is a story to bring the eight times table alive. Recite it with enthusiasm, and try drawing your own pictures!

ONE:RUN.......One octopus has to run because he is late..........LATE:EIGHT

TWO:SHOE.....Two octupuses clean every shoe...LICKS CLEAN:SIXTEEN

THREE:BRIE...eating Brie.......DO HAVE SOME MORE: TWENTY-FOUR

FOUR:DOOR......Four wait at the door...WHAT-A-QUEUE!:THIRTY-TWO

FIVE:DIVE...................Five dive into drink....................NAUGHTY:FORTY

SIX:SICK.....................Six are ill..............SIX ACHES ARE FORTY-EIGHT

SEVEN:HEAVENSeven on their way to heavenLIFTY STICKS:FIFTY-SIX

EIGHT:PLATE.....Eight drop their plates....STICKY FLOOR:SIXTY-FOUR

NINE:LINE..Nine dance in a line....SOMETHING TO DO:SEVENTY-TWO

TEN:HEN.............................Big fat hen........................WEIGHTY-EIGHTY

Further reading

Violet Brand, *Spelling Made Easy* (series of books), Egon, 1984.

Andrew W. Ellis, *Reading, Writing and Dyslexia*, Lawrence Erlbaum Associates, 1993.

Sally Raymond, *Treasure Hunt*, Henderson, 1995 (clues for treasure hunt games around the home – ideal for encouraging literacy skills).

Margaret Snowling, *Dyslexia: A Cognitive Developmental Perspective*, Blackwell, 1987.

Useful addresses

British Dyslexia Association
98 London Road
Reading RG1 5AU
Tel: 01743 668271 (from January 1998: 0118 966 8271)

Hornsby International Dyslexic Centre
Glenshee Lodge
261 Trinity Road
London SW18 3SN
Tel: 0181 877 9737

Dyspraxia Foundation
8 West Alley
Hitchin
Hertfordshire SG5 1EG
Tel: 01462 454986

LADDER (National Learning and Attention Deficit Disorders
Association)
Bookshop: PO Box 590/Information: PO Box 700
Wolverhampton WV3 7YY
Tel: 01902 336272

Educational Kinesiology Foundation UK (founded Brain Gym)
12 Golders Rise
Hendon
London NW4 2HR
Tel: 0181 202 9747

Osteopath Information Service (list of therapists and advice)
PO Box 2074
Reading
Berkshire RG1 4YR
Tel: 01734 512051

Teaching Reading Through Spelling (the Kingston Programme)
TRTS Publishing
PO Box 1349
Wrexham
Clwyd LL14 4ZA
Tel: 01978 840868

The Listening Library (stories on tape)
12 Lant Street
London SE1 1QH
Tel: 0171 407 9417
(asks for annual subscription plus confirmation of necessity)

For free copy of the educational 'Code of Practice' telephone: 0181
533 2000

The Dyslexic Computer Resource Centre
Department of Psychology
University of Hull
Hull HU6 7RX
Please send a large SAE to receive information about computer
software.

Index

Attention Deficit Hyperactive
Disorder (ADHD) 72–3
audio memory weakness 70,
74–5

Christopher 5, 7, 8
Clare 3–4, 6–7, 70–1
clumsiness 4, 16; games 46;
sport 11
computers: advantages 14;
games 11, 45
contextual prompting 8, 20–1

dyslexia: as 'specific learning
difficulty' 61–3; defining 1;
discussing with child 17, 18,
79, 83; how common? 84;
improving memory skills
73–6; physiological features
68–9; psychologist's
assessment 58–61; symptoms
1–2; types of memory
weakness 69–72
dyspraxia 16

educational psychologists 57;
individual assessment and
report 58–61
emotional conflicts: at home
10–12; case studies 3–6;
cultivating self-esteem and
confidence 61–3; games 43–4,
45–6; individually 83;
motivation to learn 80

family: grandparents and
siblings 17–18

games 43–6; cards 44, 46–7;
computers 11, 45; dice 45,
47–9; emotional conflict 43–4,
45–6; mathematics 93;
memory use 49–51, 77–8;
quizzes and general
knowledge 85–7; spelling
32–4, 35–6, 44–5, 85, 89–91;
words 26

handwriting 4, 37–8
health: holistic health and
specialist approaches 58;
tiredness 25
hobbies and interests 14–15;
acting and drama club 65;
children in wider world 65–7;
stamp collecting 3, 6, 14
home life: difficulties in
everyday life 10–12; hobbies
14–16; homework 15–16, 40;
organizational skills 12–14;
reading time and materials 22
homework: extra support at
home 40; helping 53, 54–5;
supporting 15–16

Jonathan 4, 6–7

Mark 4, 7, 8, 72
mathematics 39–42;
Christopher's case 5, 8, 9,

18–19; games 47–9, 93
memory 68–70; aids and tactics 77–8; audio weakness 70, 74–5; games 49–51; improving performance 73–4; multisensory approach 76; semantic weakness 71, 75; utilizing strengths 76–7; visual weakness 70–1, 75; working memory weakness 72, 75–6
motivation 80
multisensory approach 76

organizational skills 12–14; clocks and calendars 13

reading 20–2; access 25–6; building confidence 26–7; case studies 4–7; common word list 91–2; decoding words 21, 23; defining words while reading 24; eyesight and good health 24–5; identifying particular weakness 22; perceived as 'boring' 11; phonological approach 6; positive outlook and confidence 79–80; signs and notices in wider world 64–5; specialist support 58; time and materials at home 22; together 22–4

Samantha 4–5, 7, 8–9, 70
schools 2; assessing the school 52–3; Code of Practice 55–7; homework 54–5; other children 53–4; outside

teaching support 57–8; report from educational psychologist 58–61; special educational needs coordinator 53, 55; teachers 53; terminology 57
self-esteem and confidence 81–3
semantic weakness 70, 75
siblings: games 43–4
signs and notices 64–5
social life 11 see also emotional conflicts; coping with teasing 54; helping children with a wider world 64–7; labelling child 67
special educational needs coordinator 53, 55
spelling see also memory: common word list 91–2; expectations and compensations 36–7, 80; games 32–4, 35–6, 85, 89–91; history and patterns in English 30–1; homophones 36; identifying weakness 29–30; lessons at home 34–5; memory tabs 32; phonological versus visual 28–30
sports 66

tape recorders: pen pals and hobbies 15
teachers: homework 15–16, 53; specialist support 57–8
time: decoding clocks and calendars 13, 86–9
Tom 5–6, 8

visual aids 6–7; memory weakness 70, 75